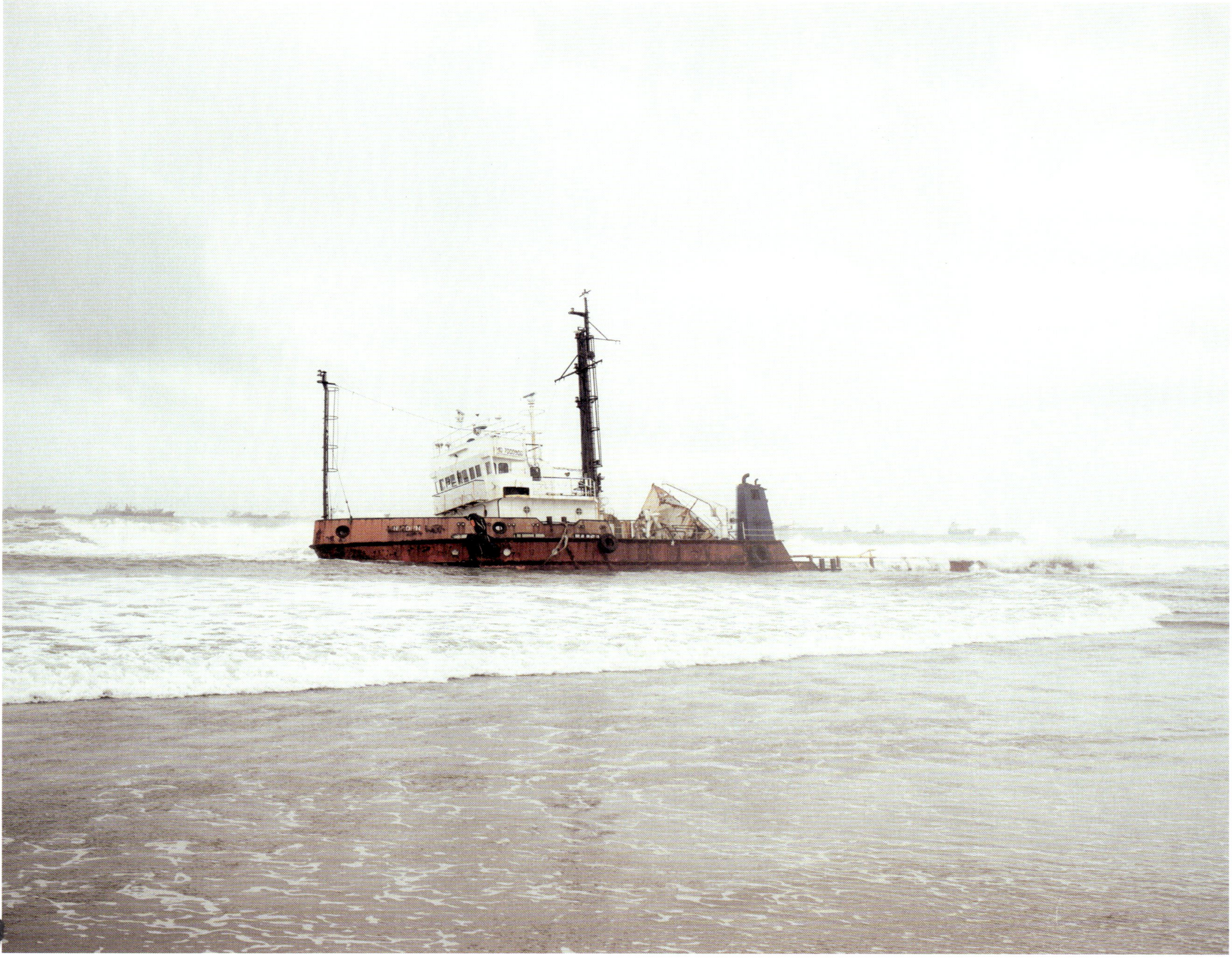

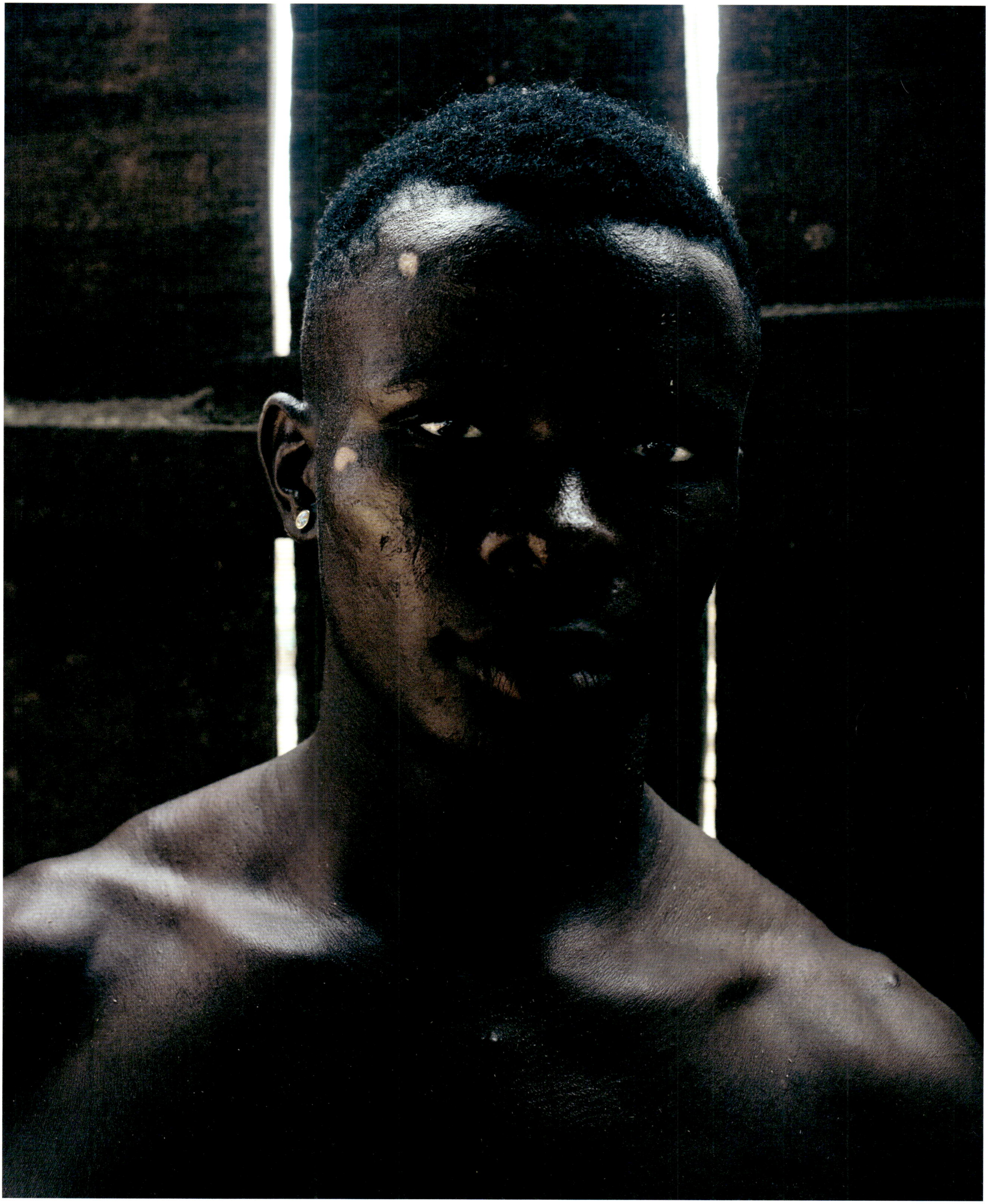

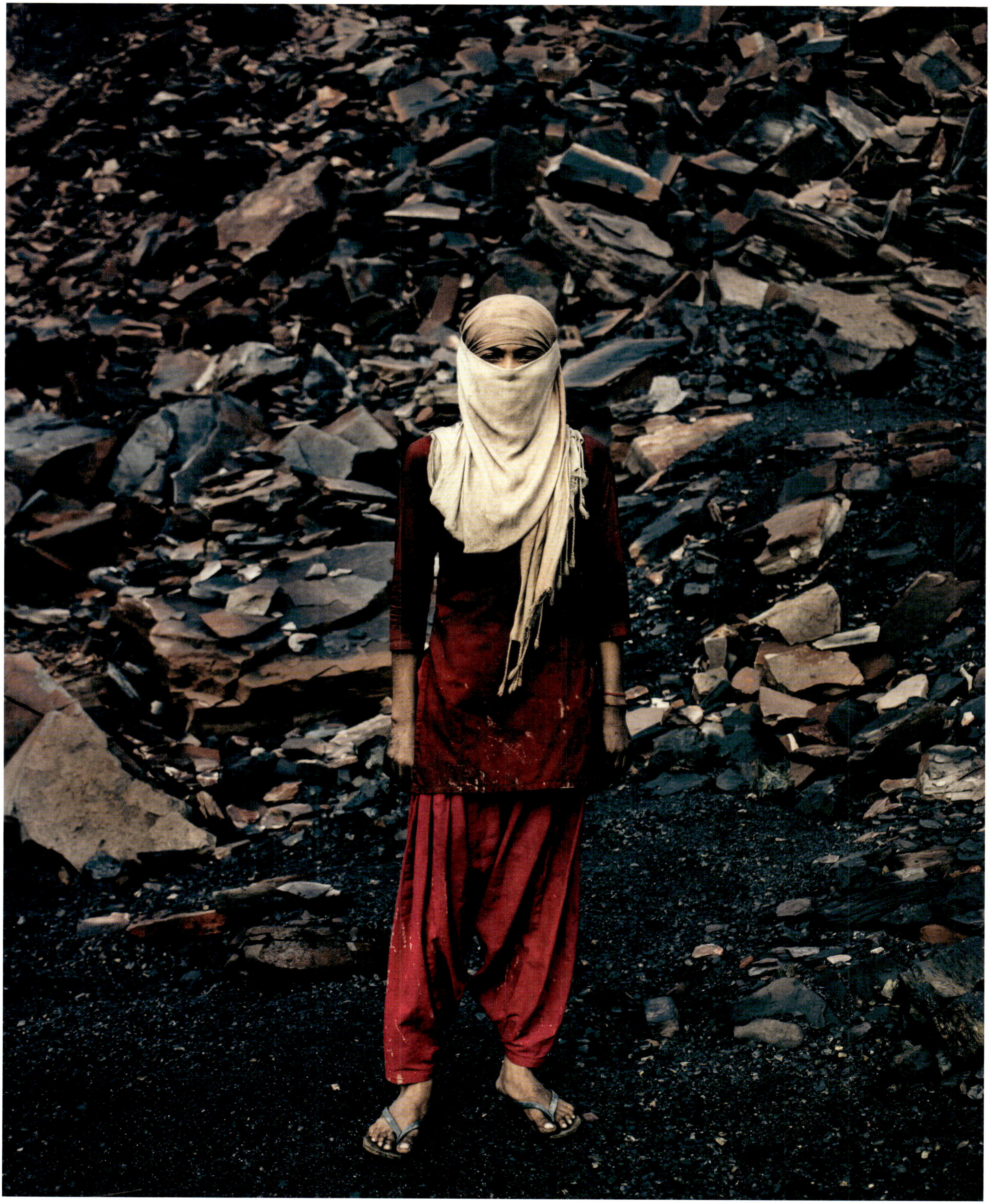

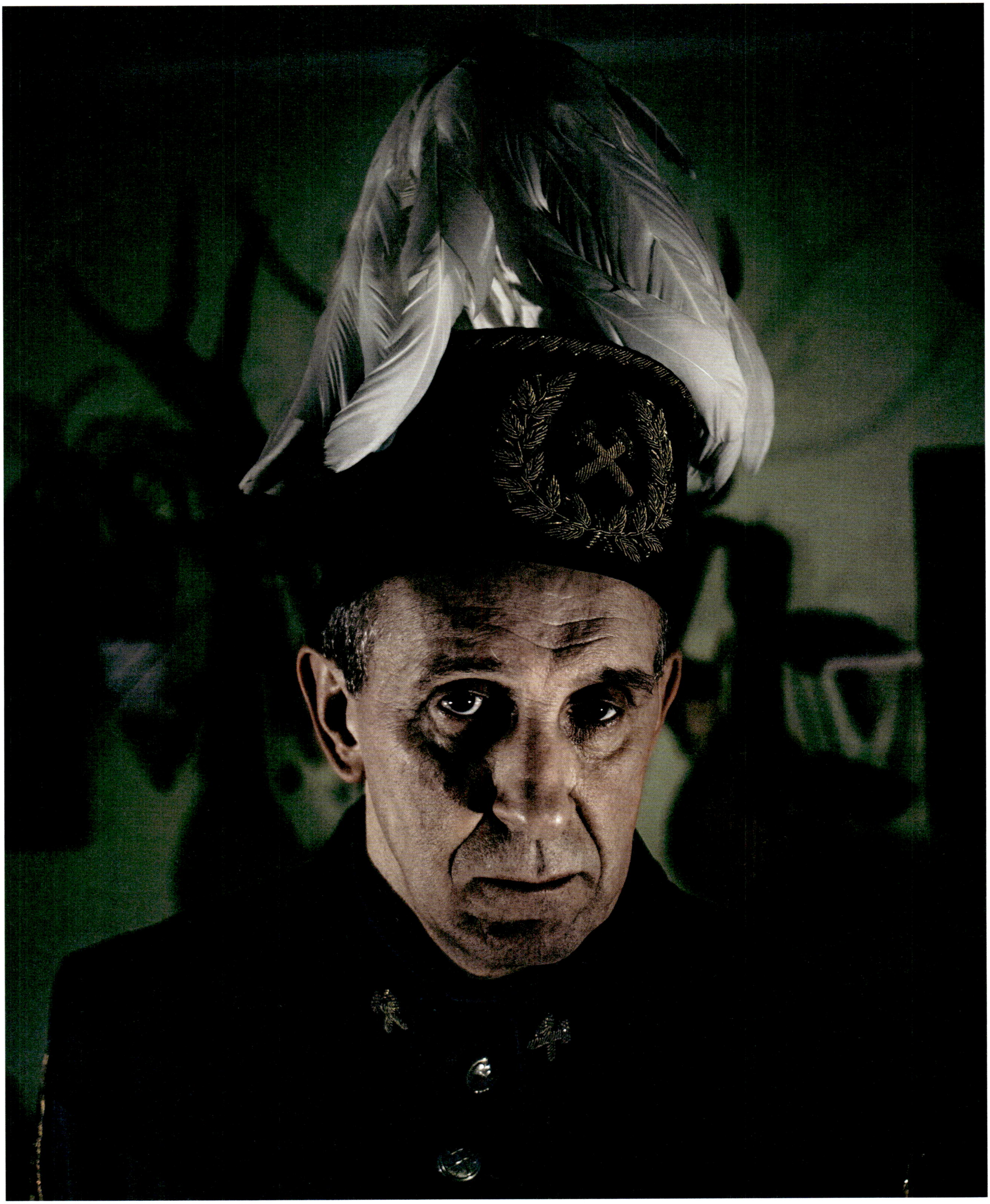

Wahala

Robin
Hinsch

GOST

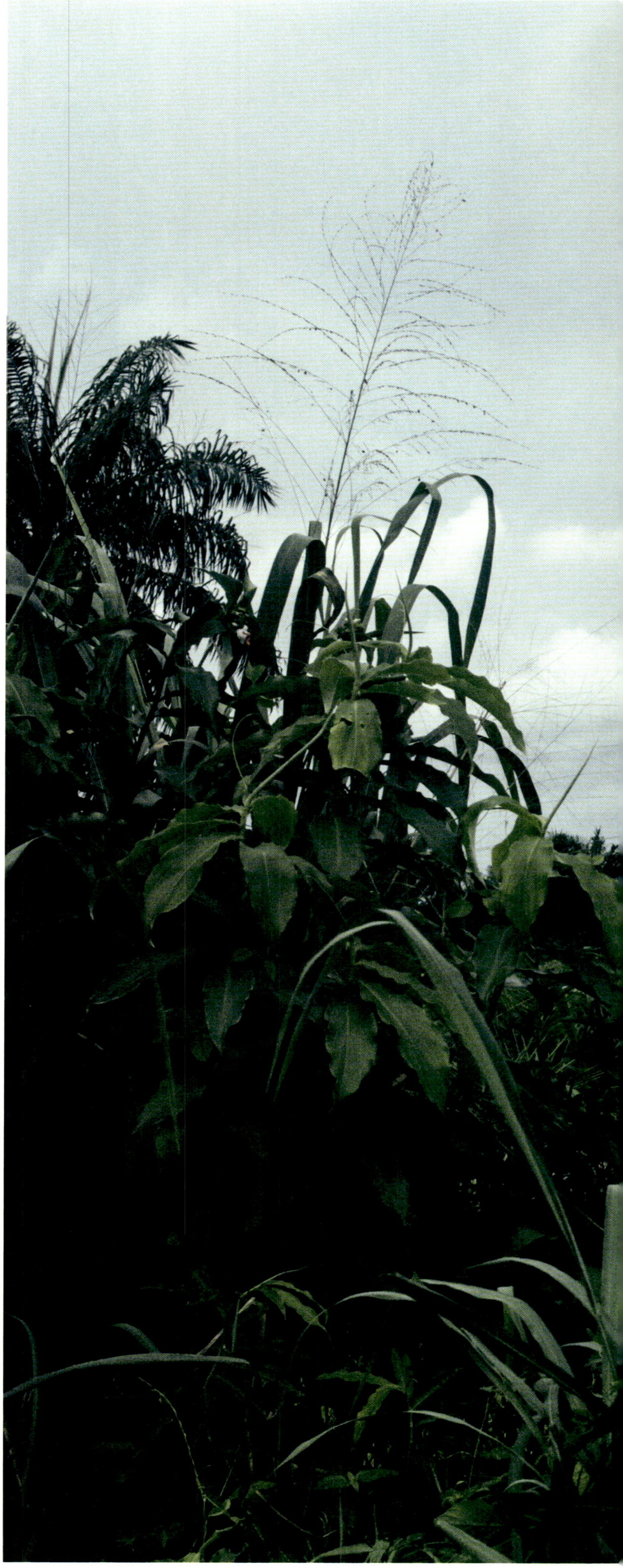

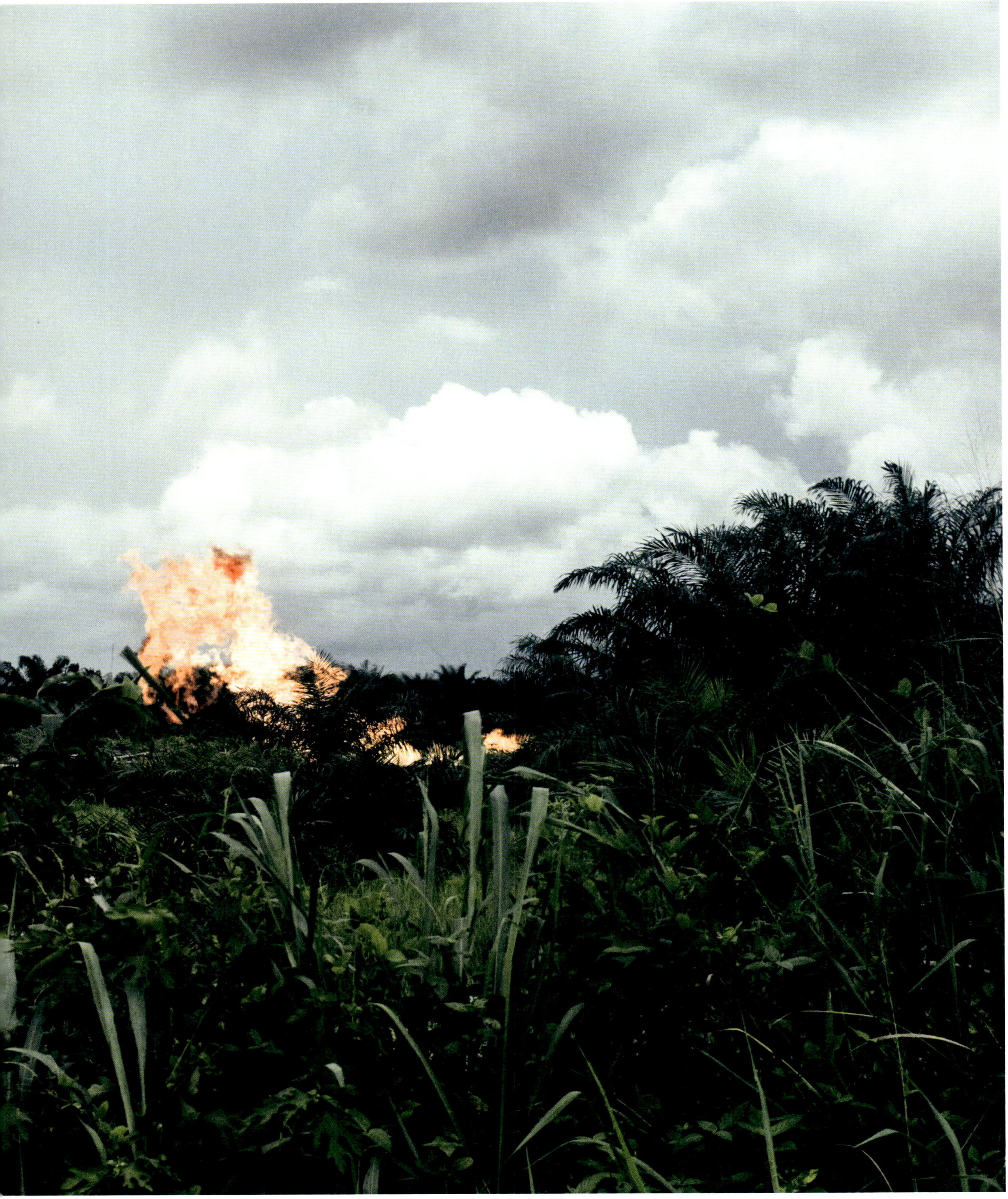

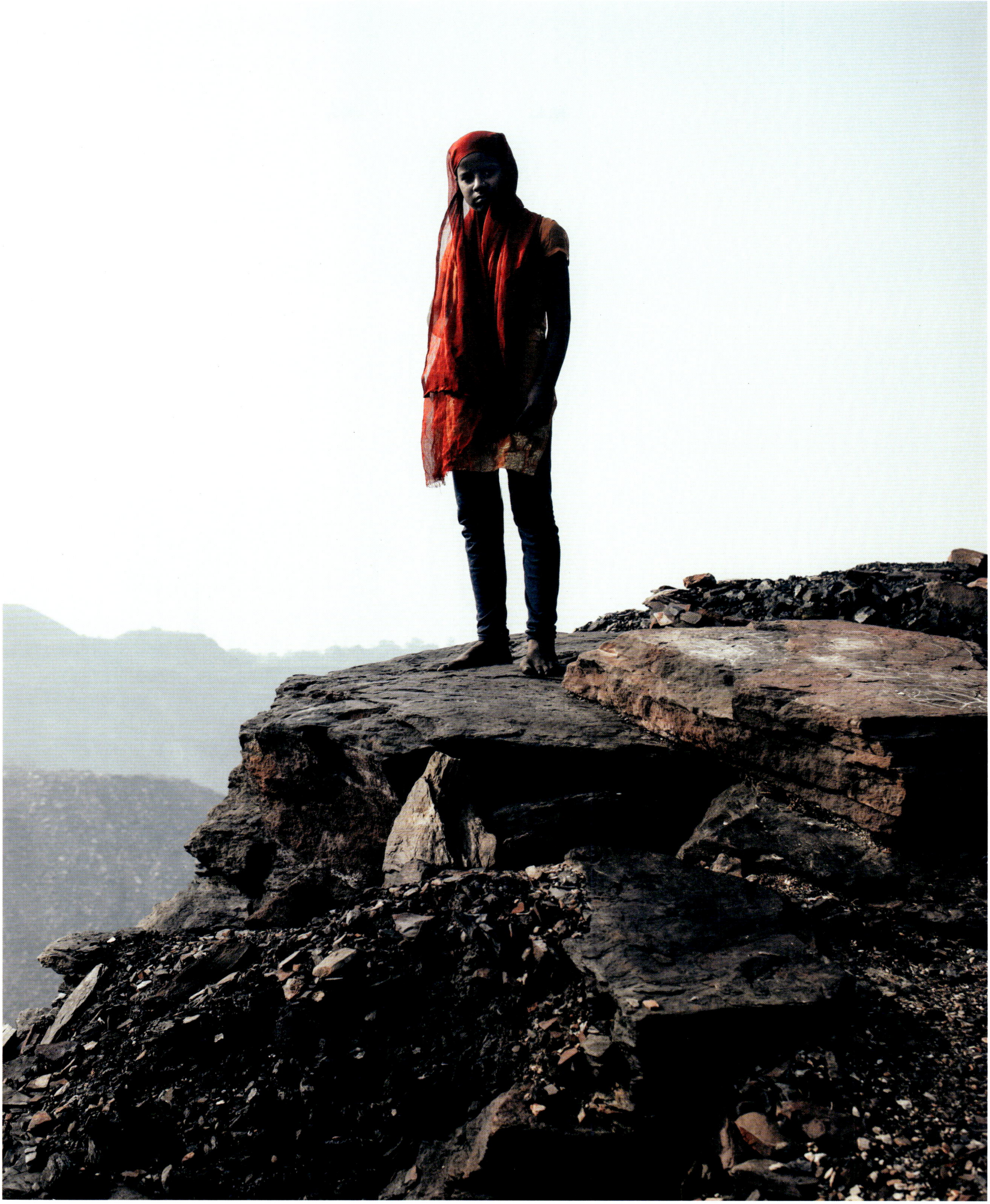

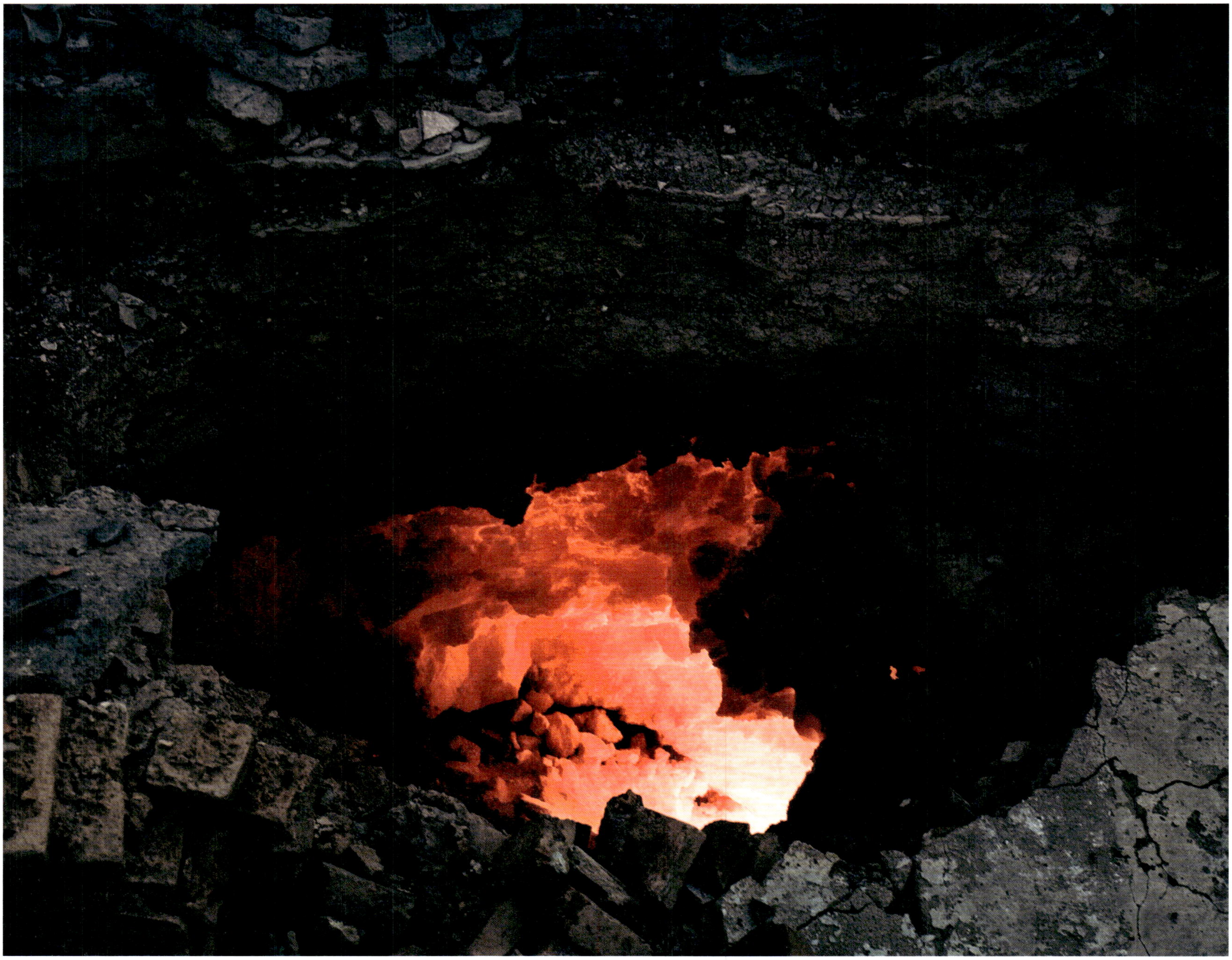

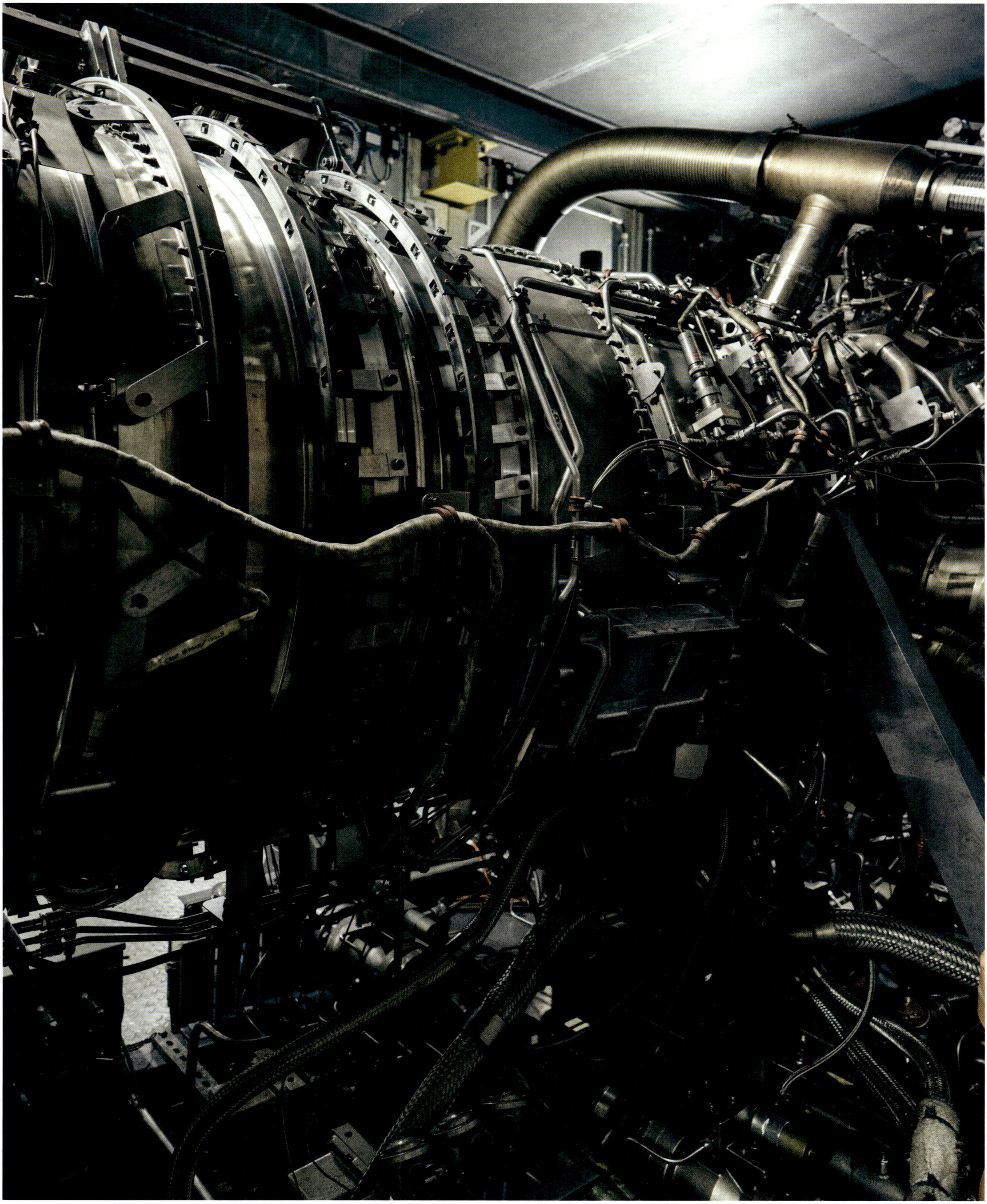

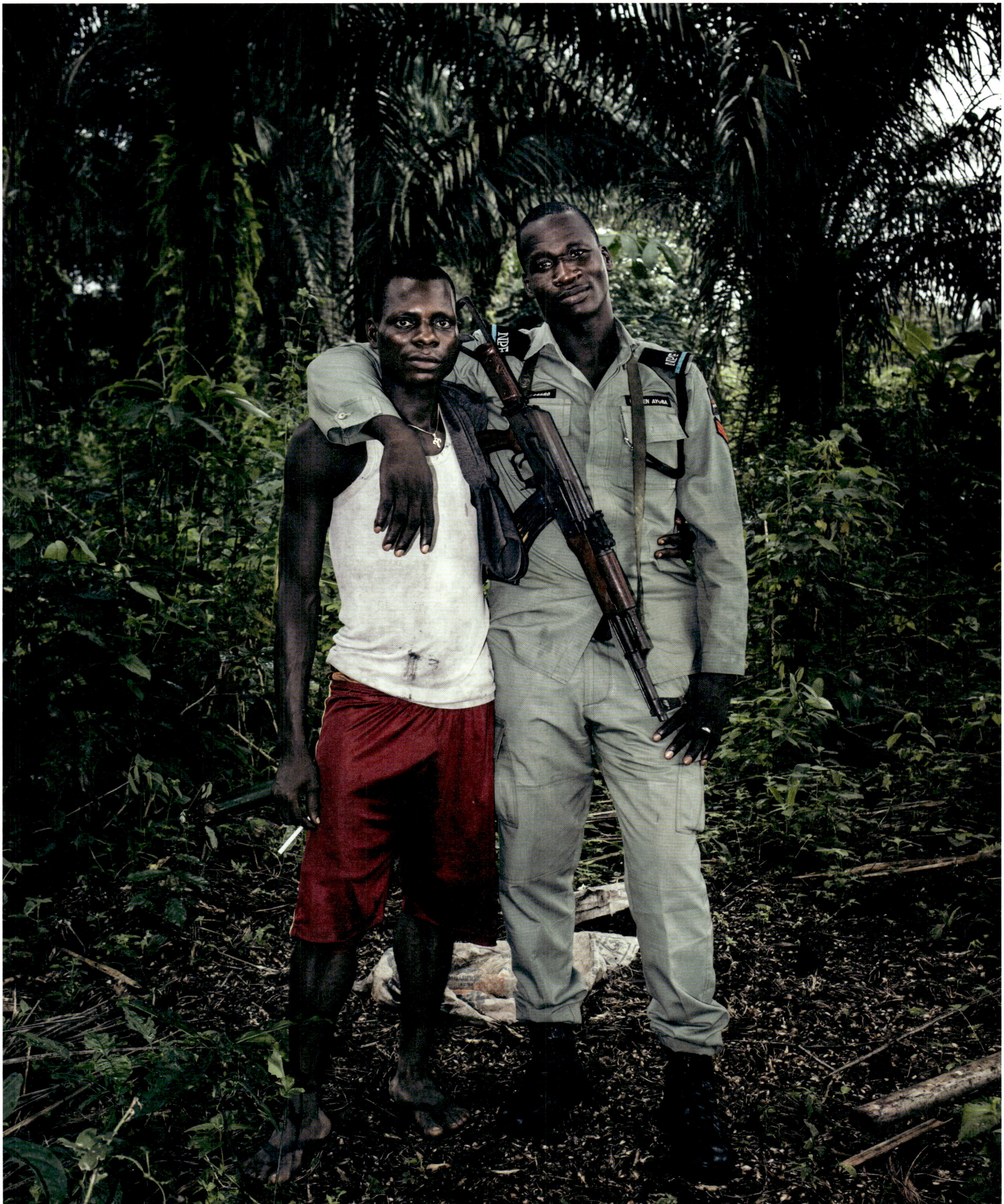

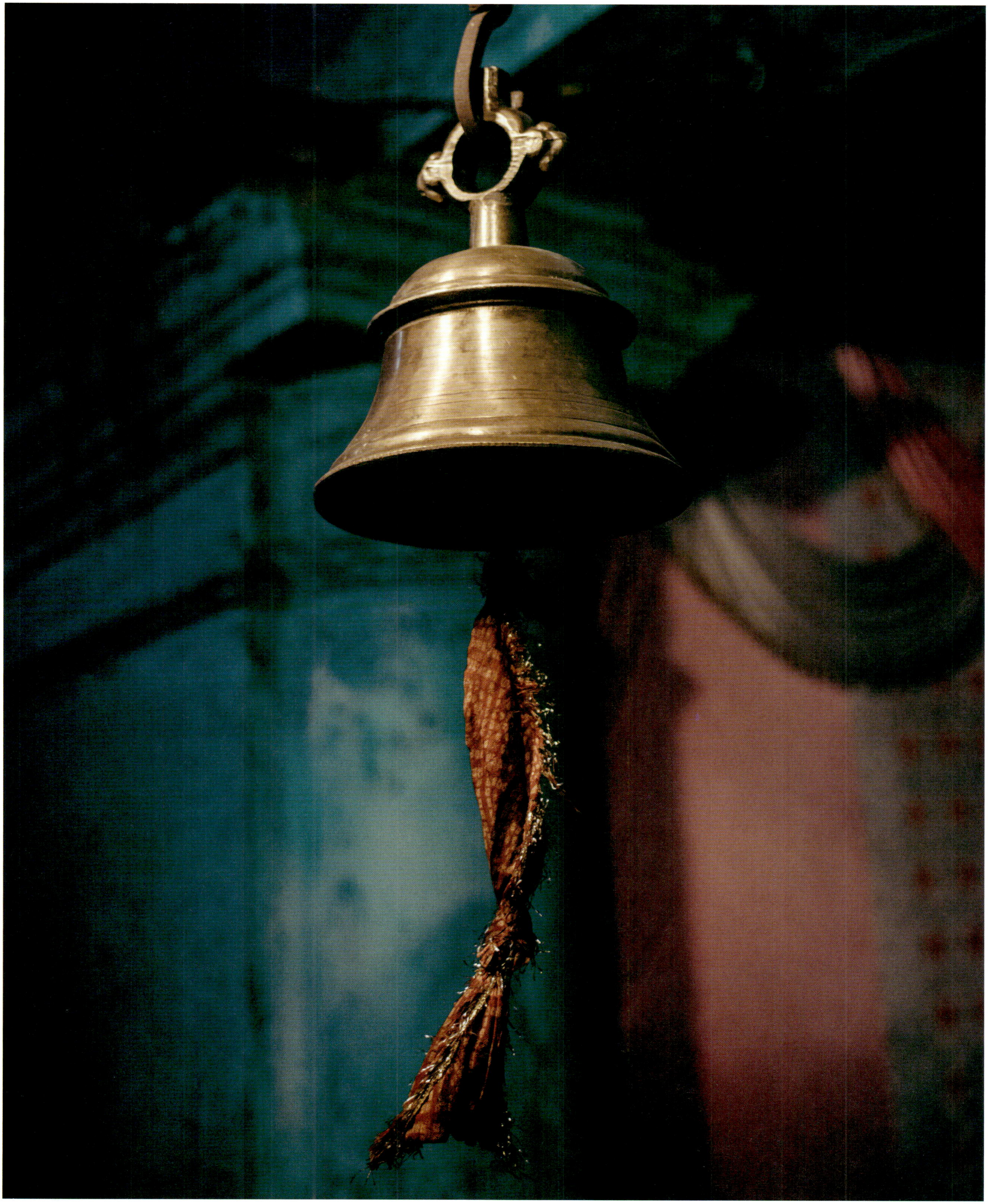

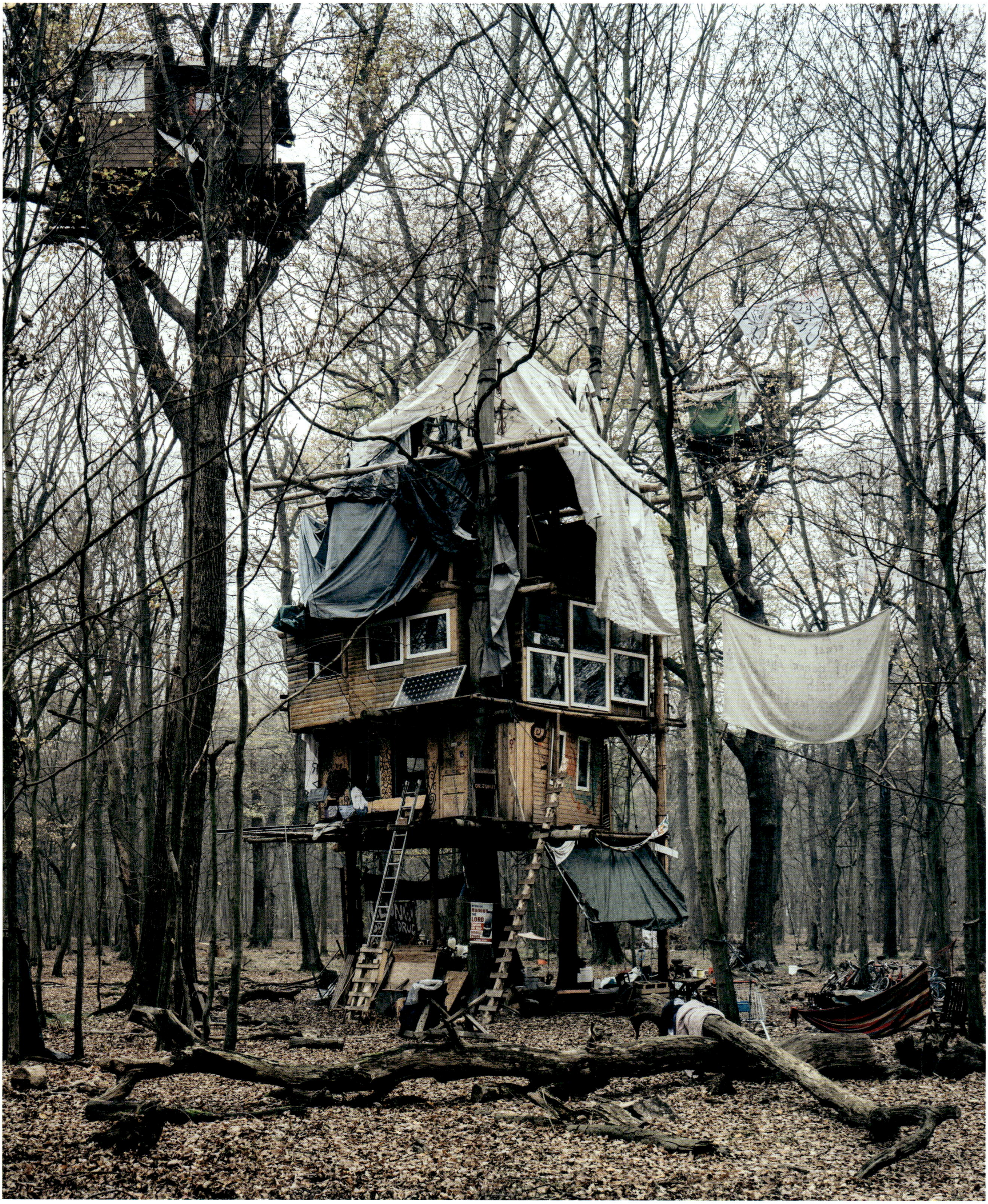
THE
LORD

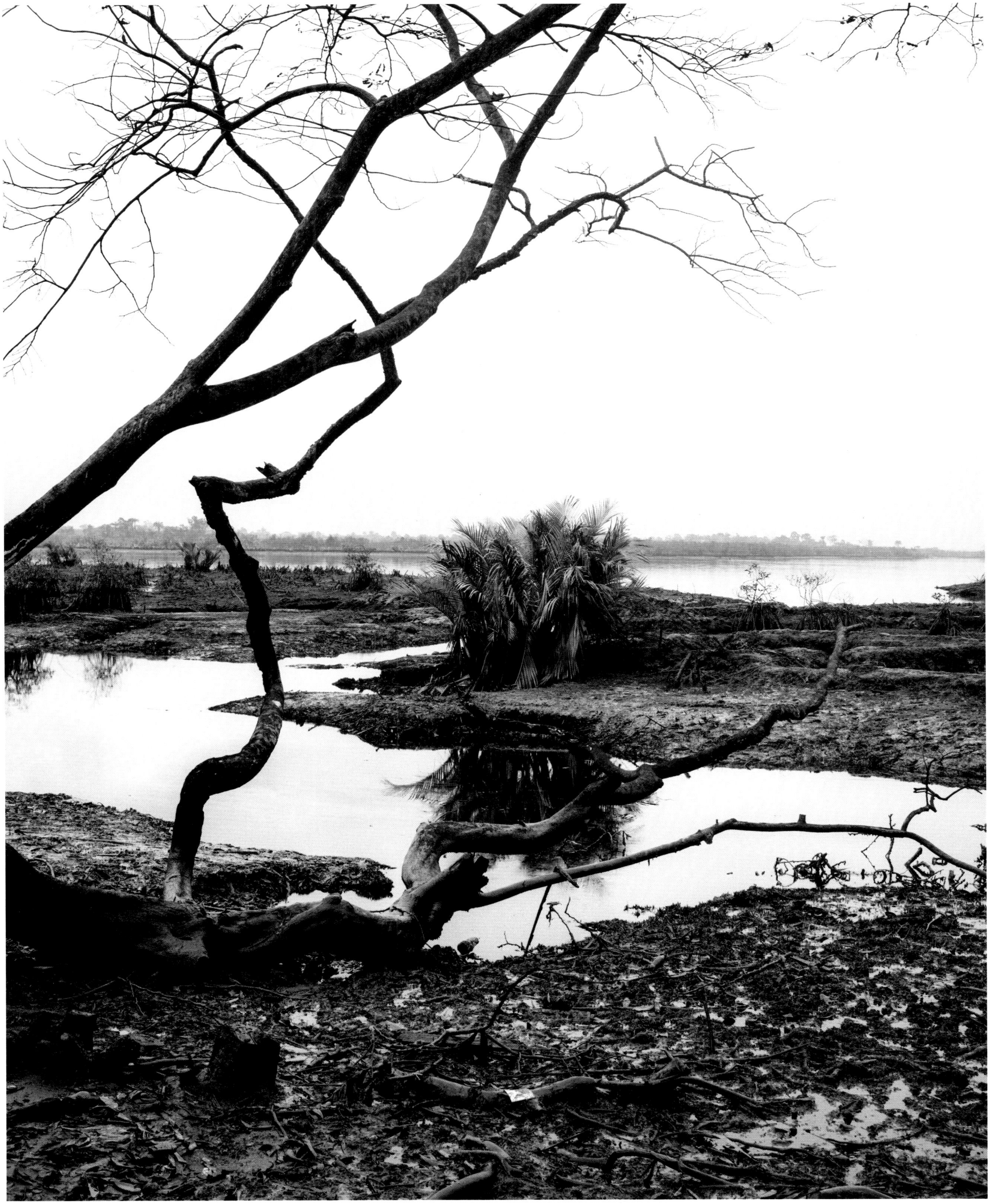

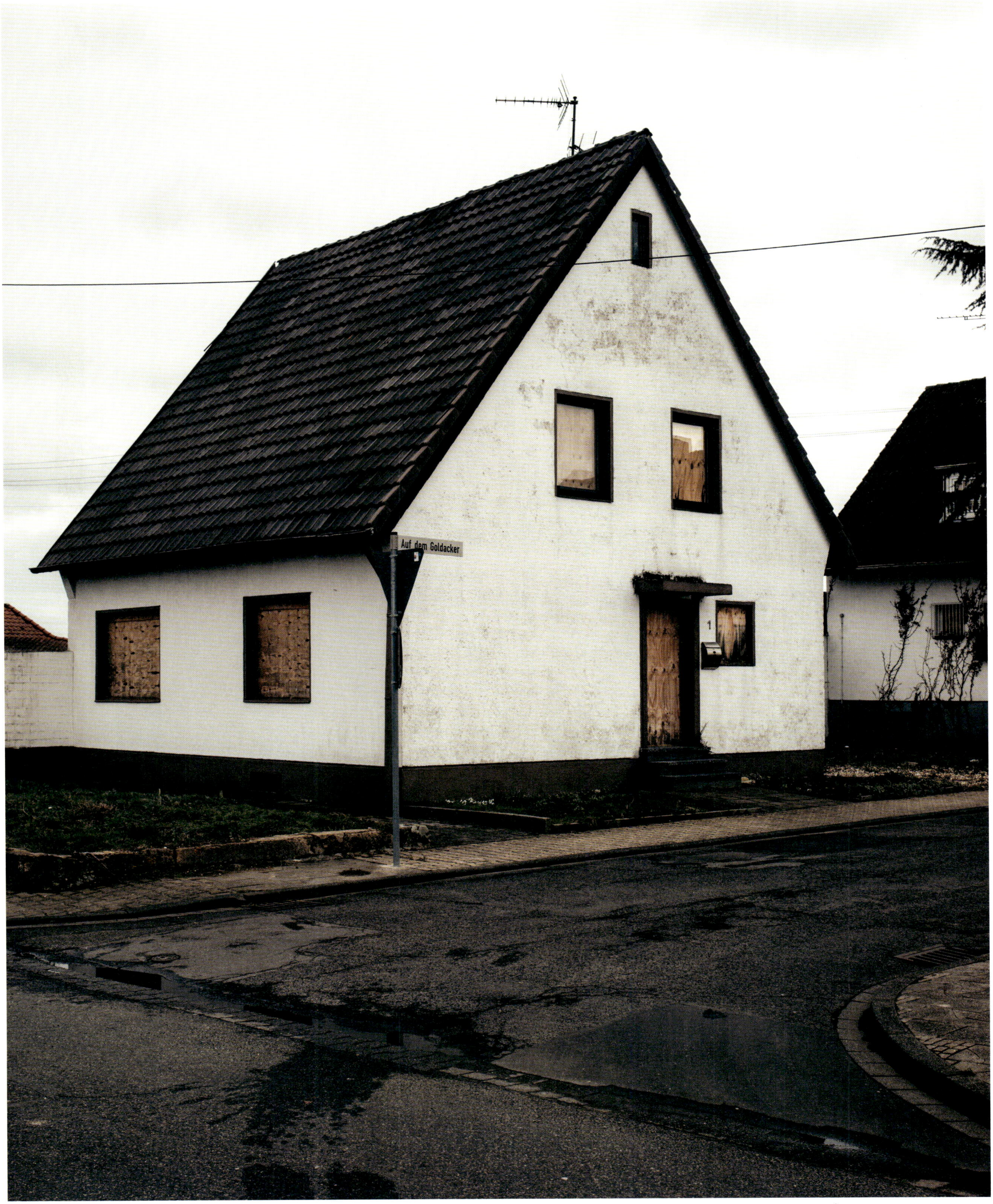
Auf dem Goldacker
1

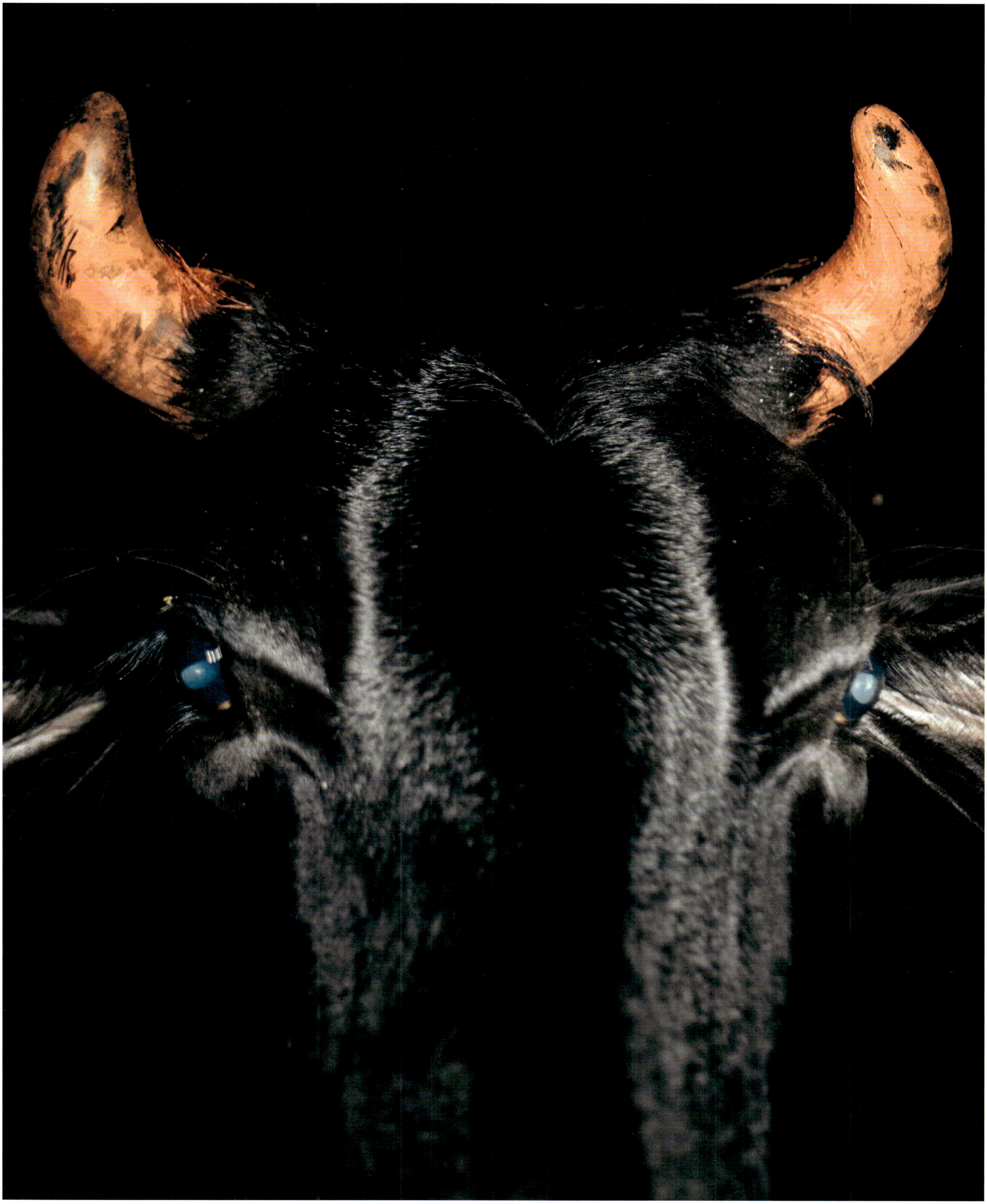

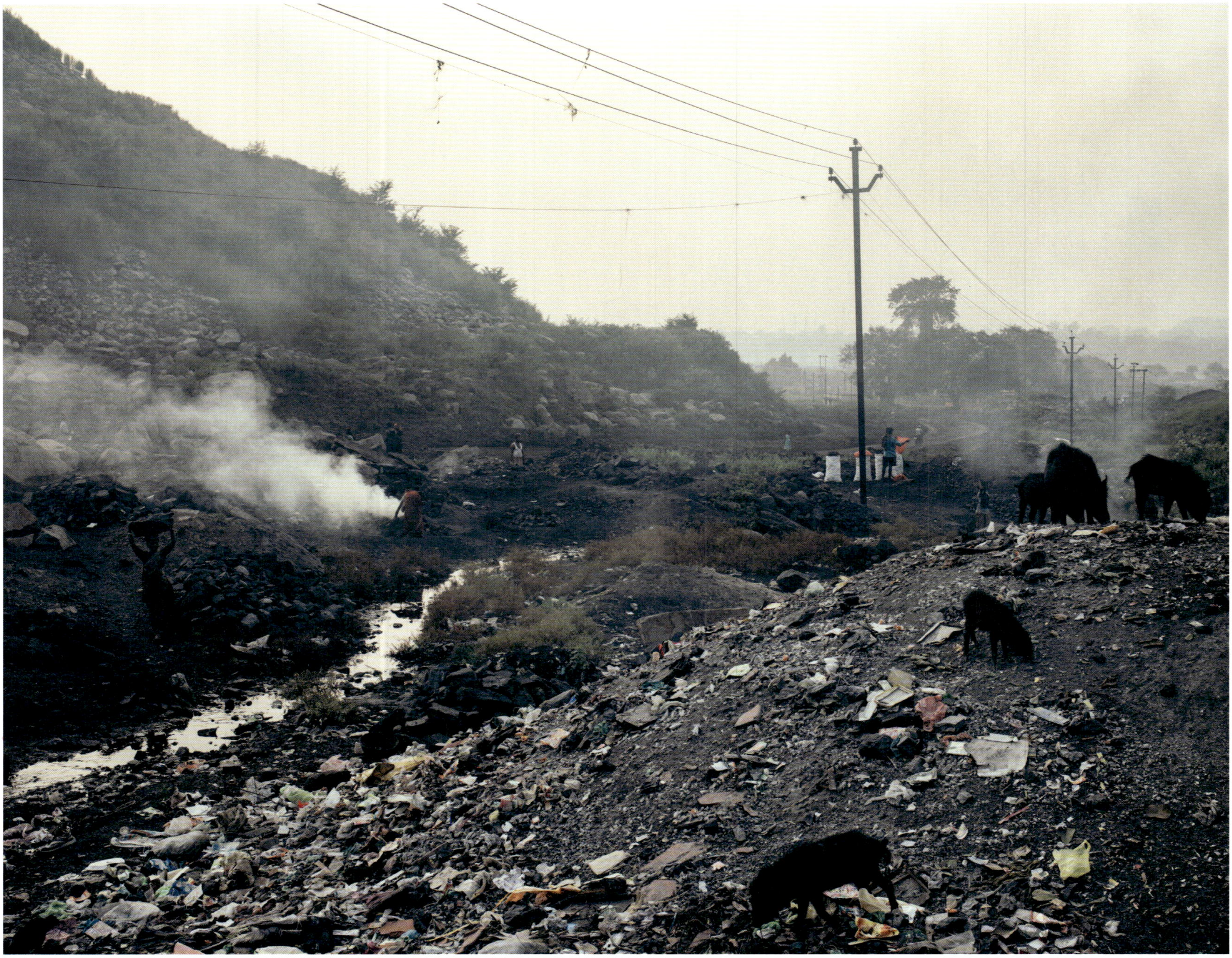

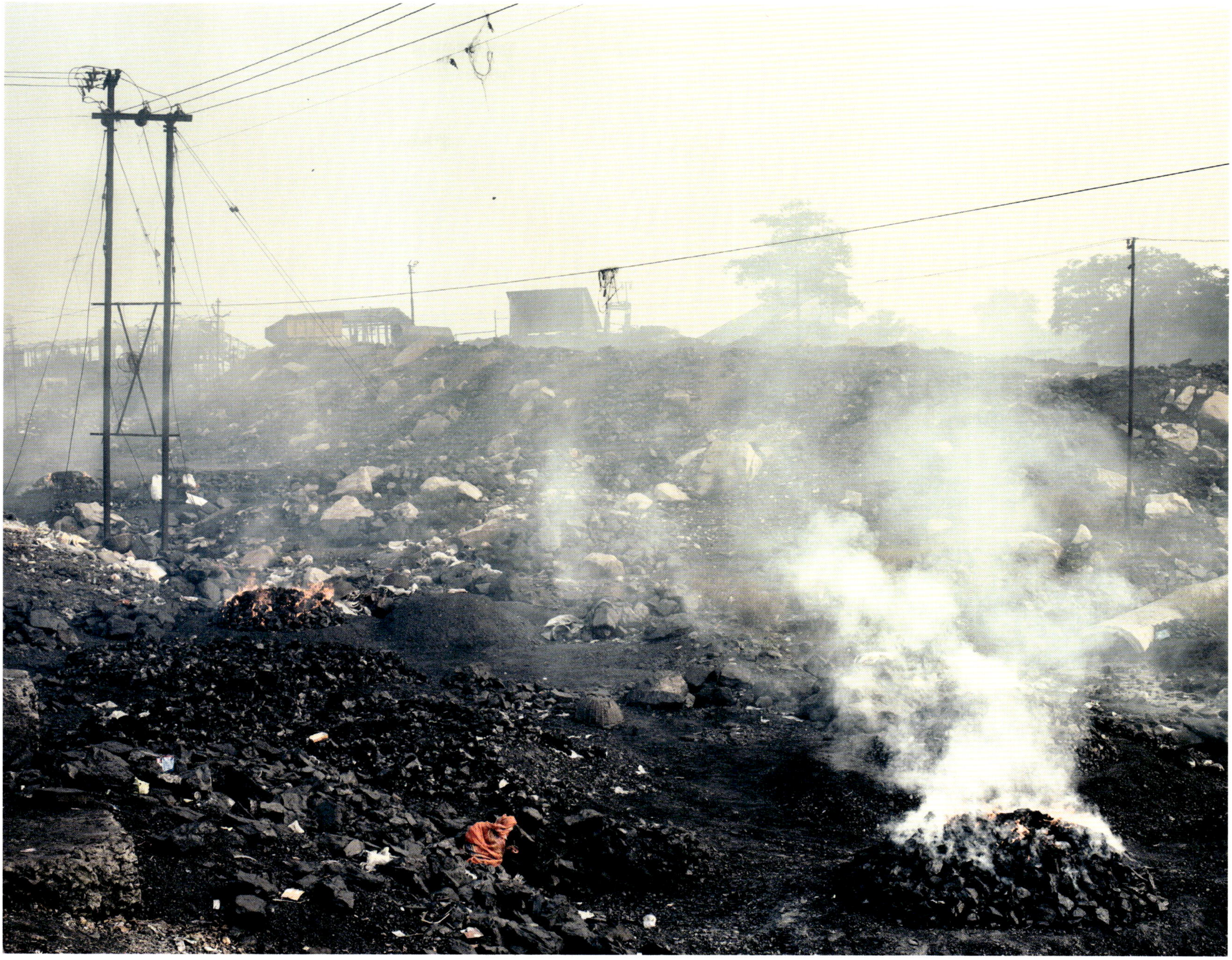

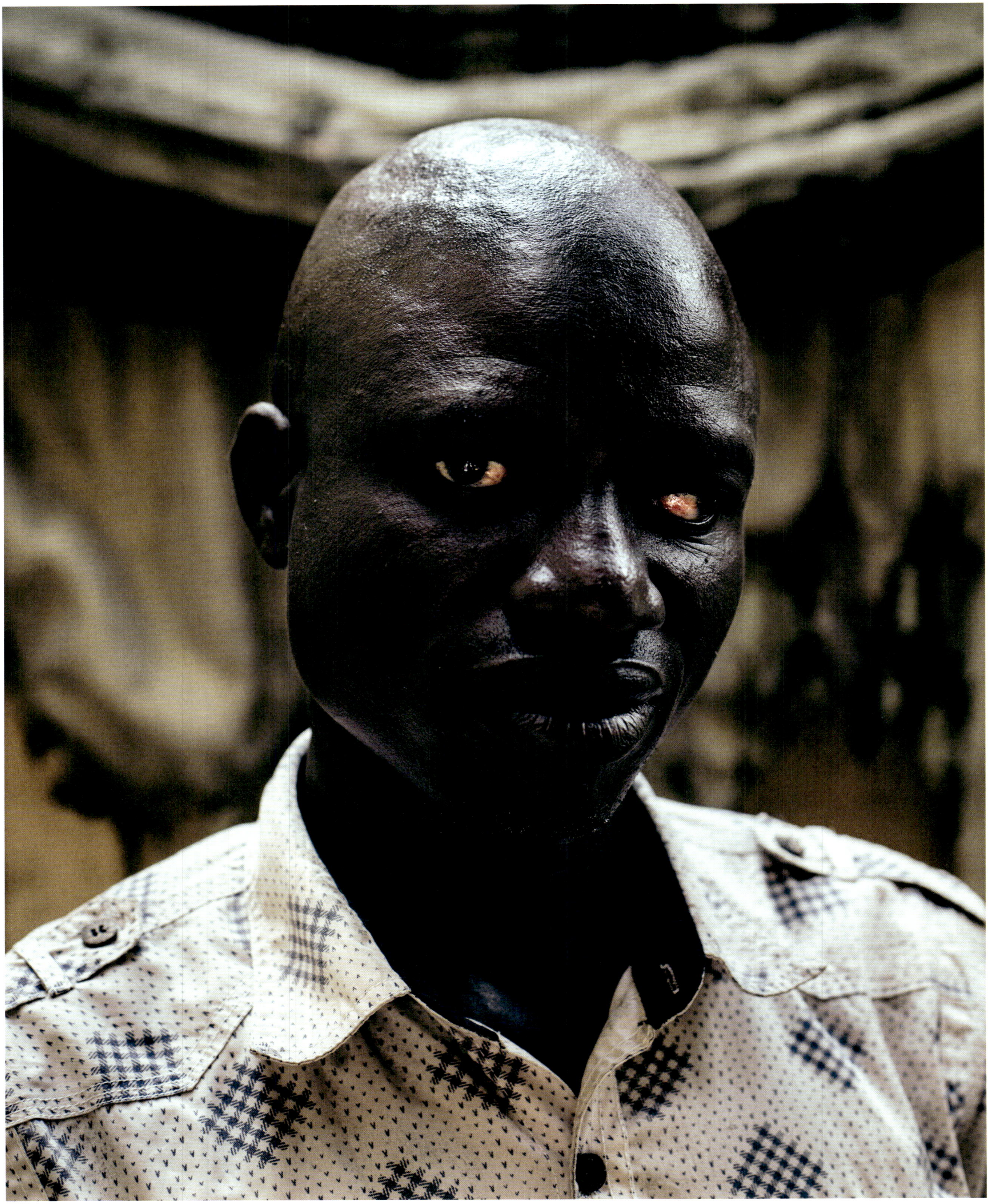

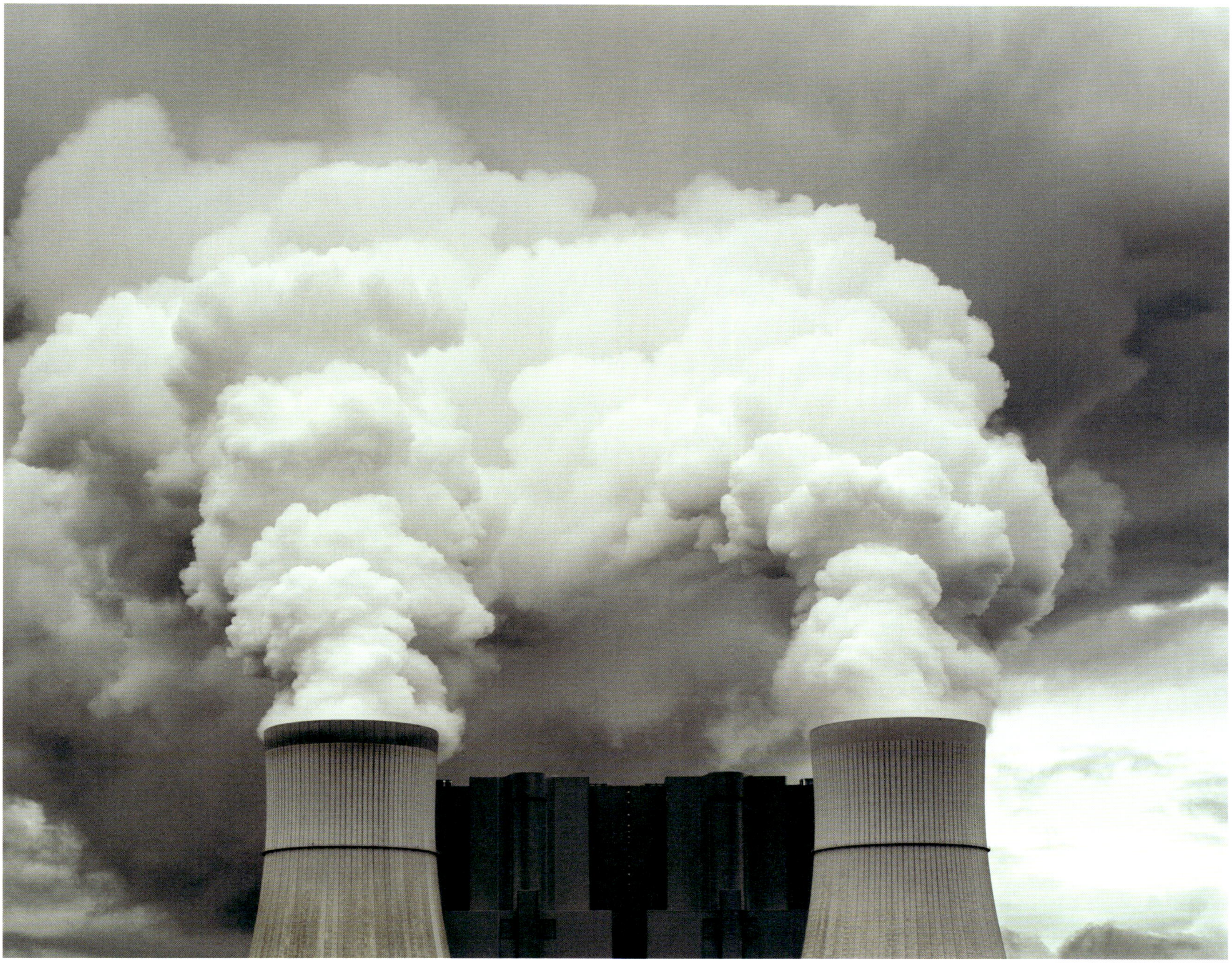

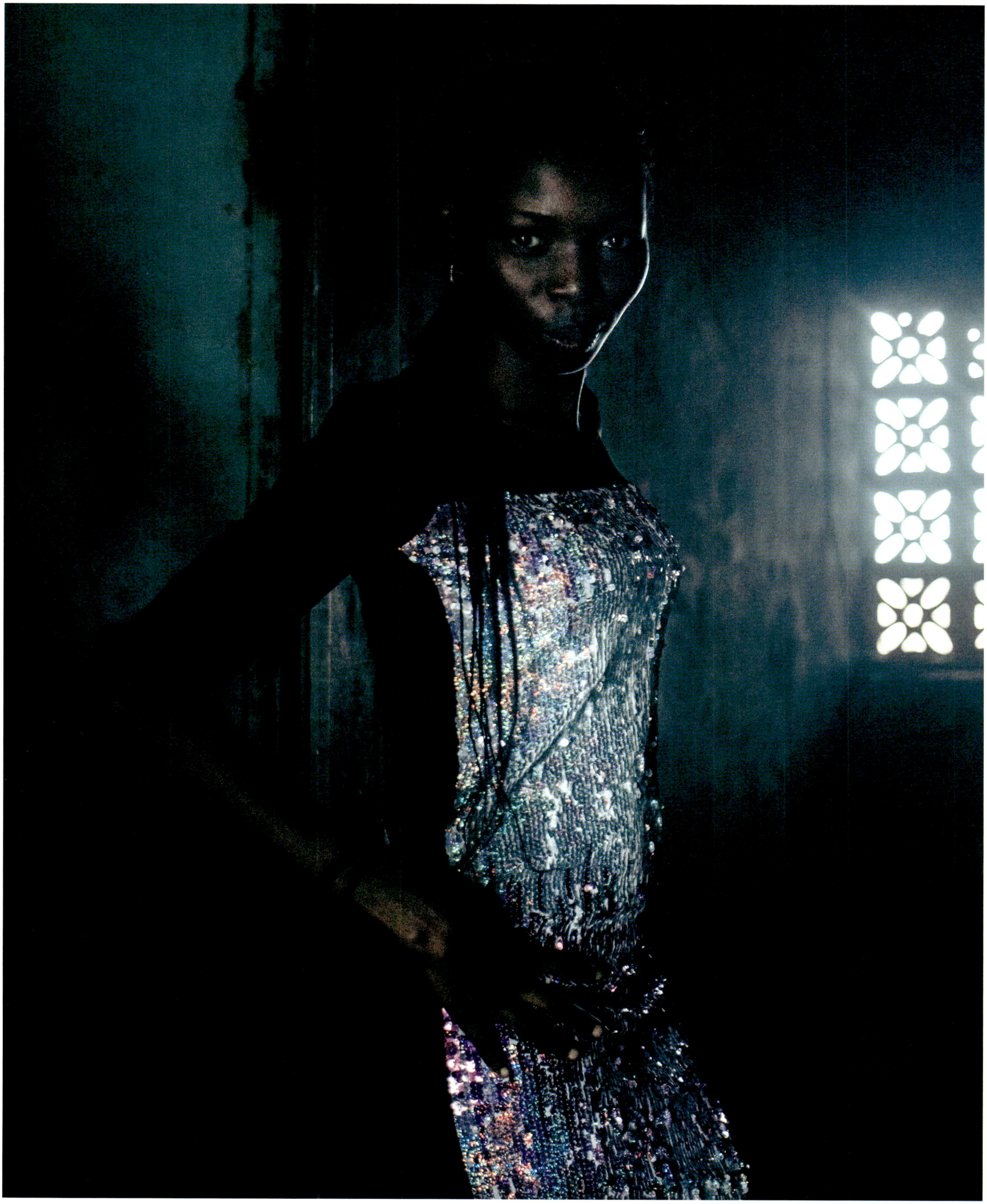

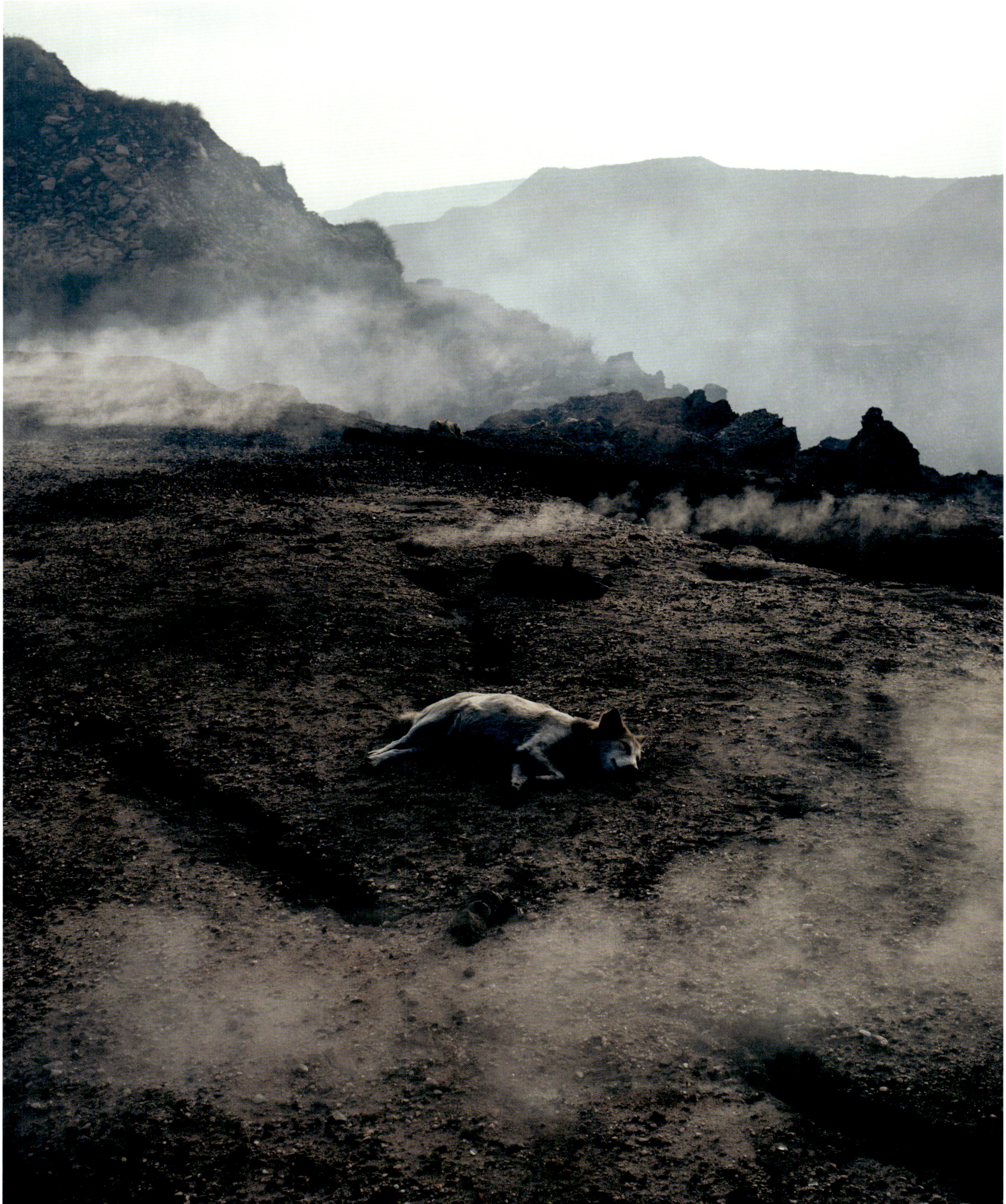

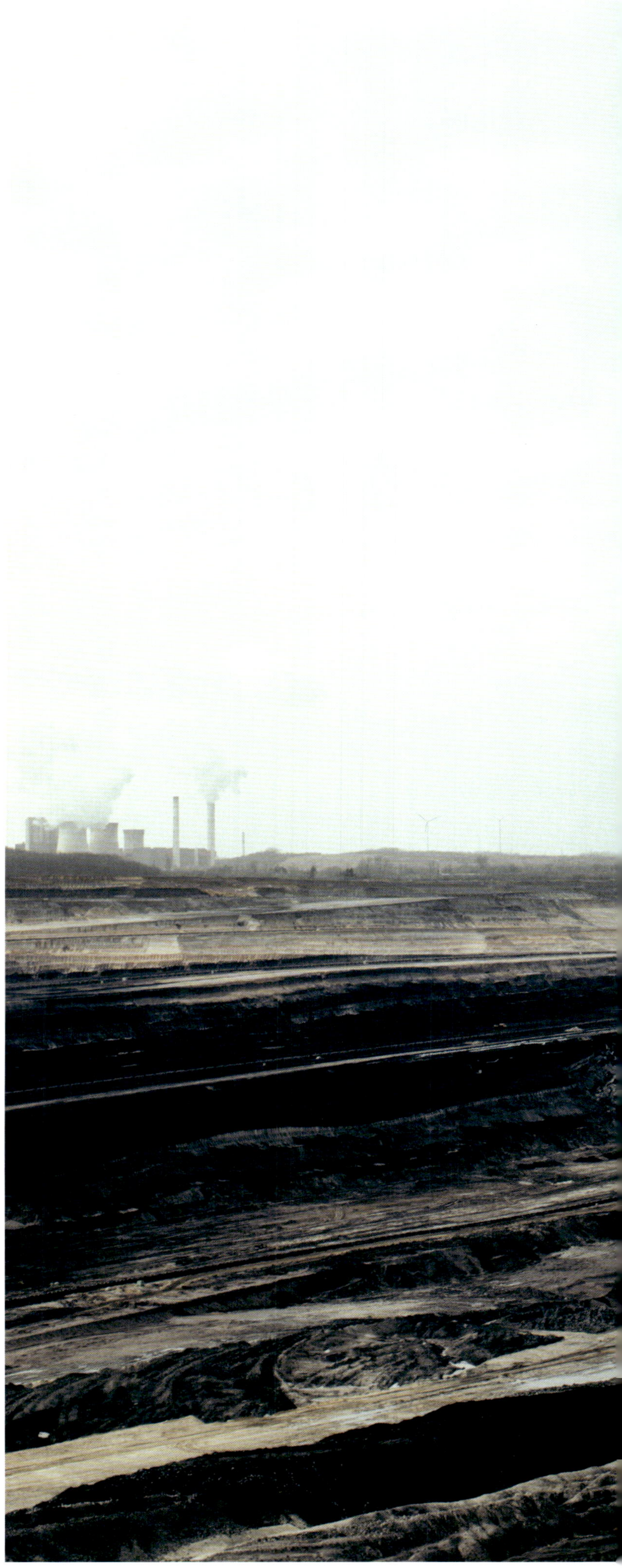

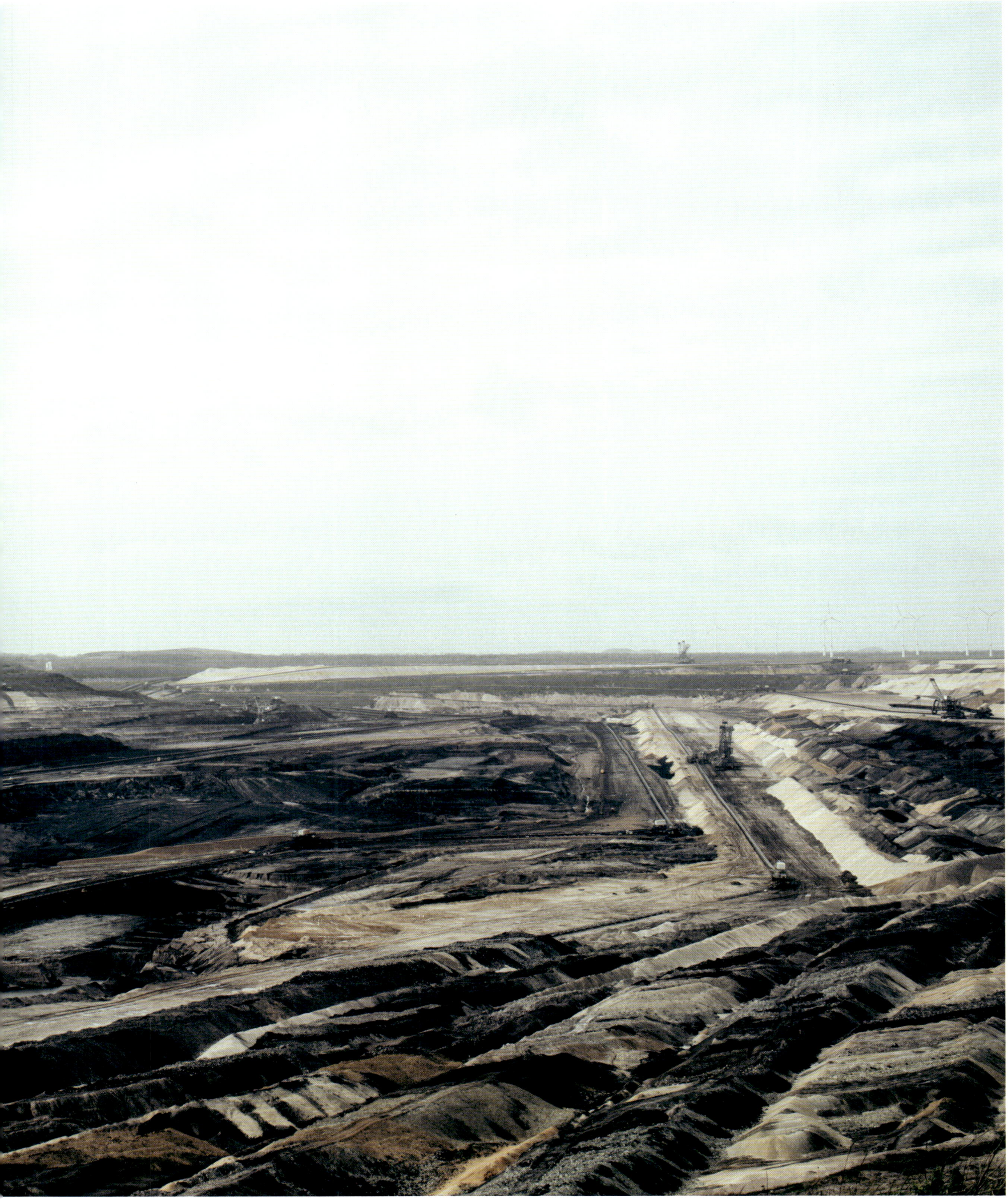

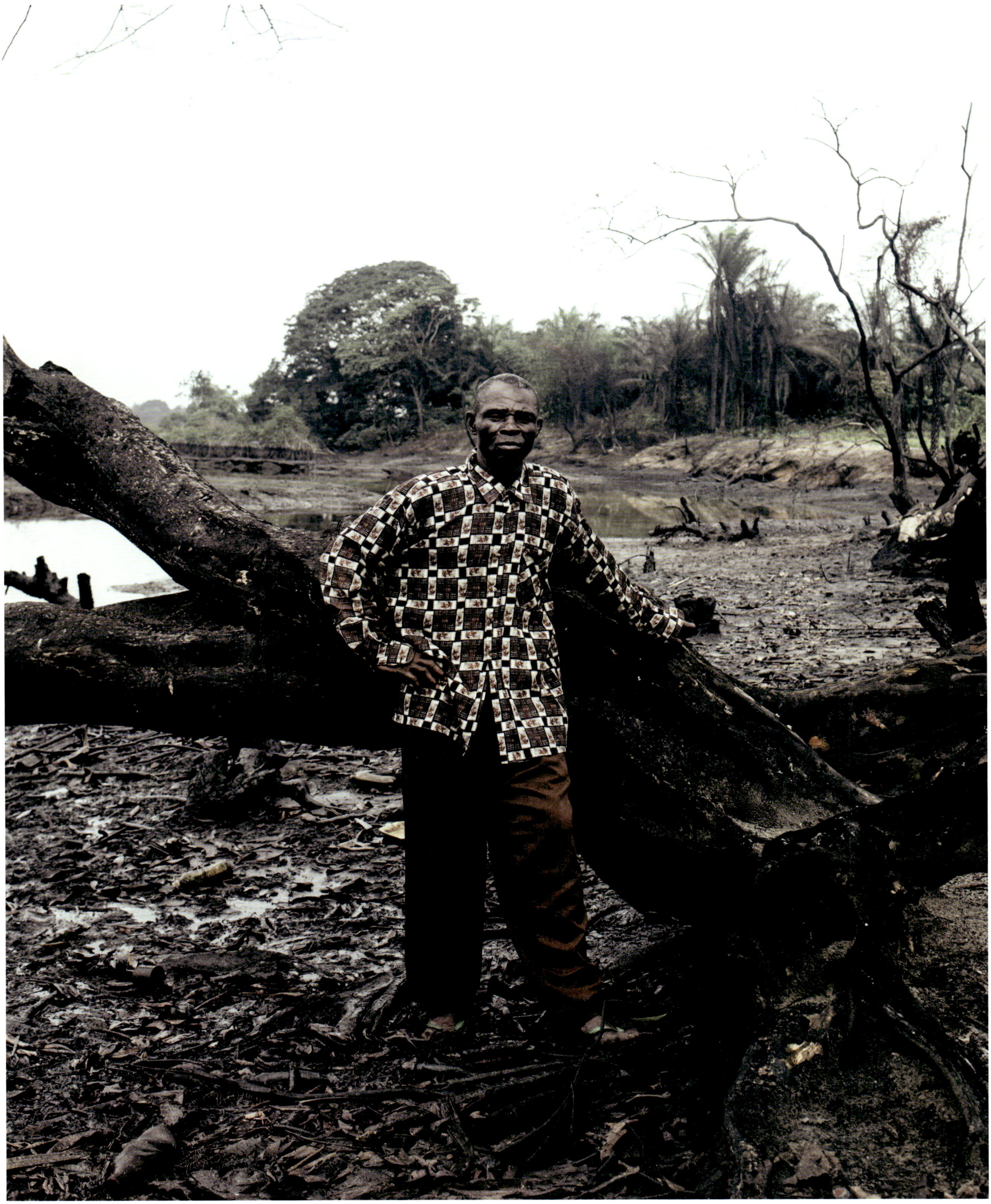

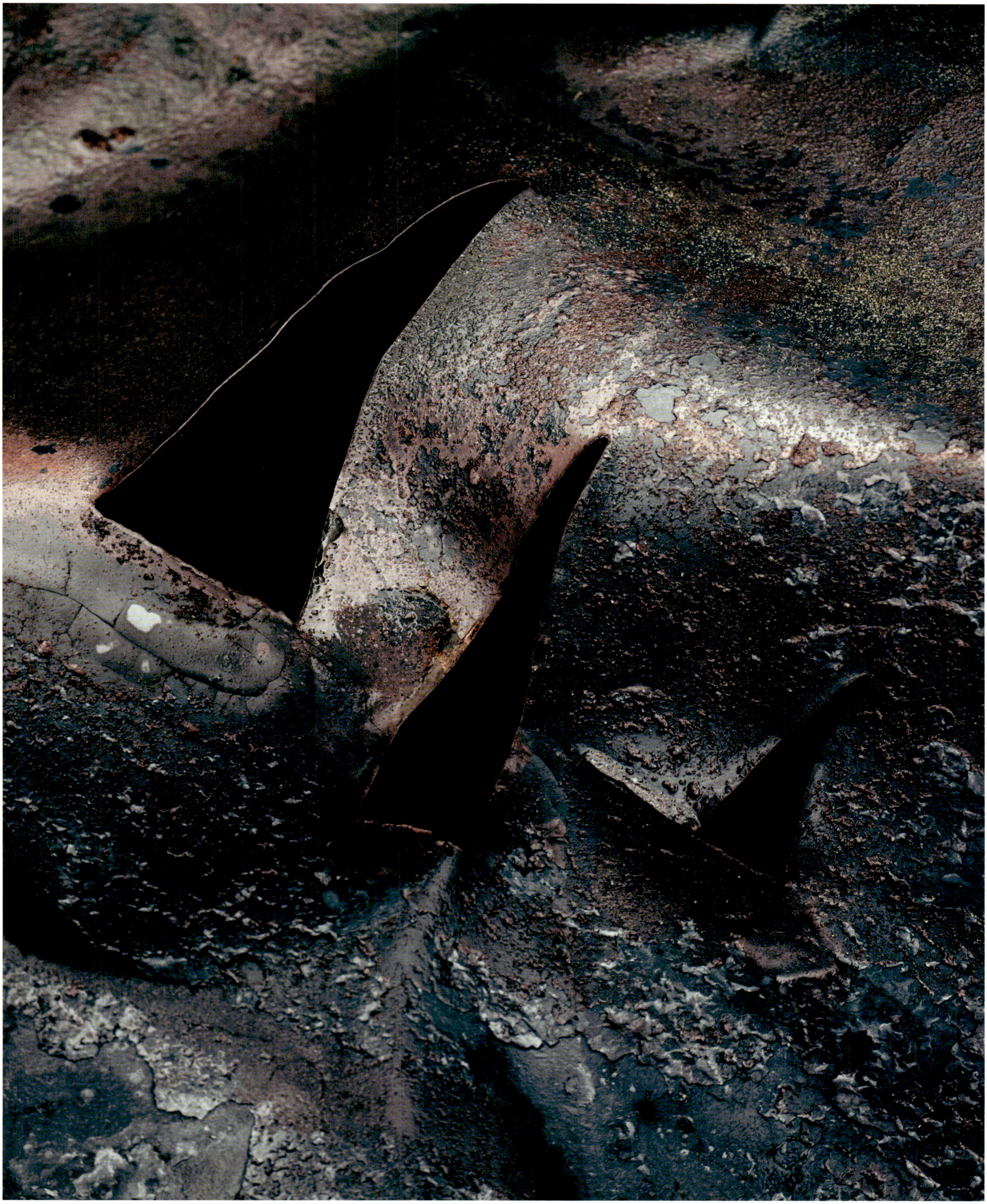

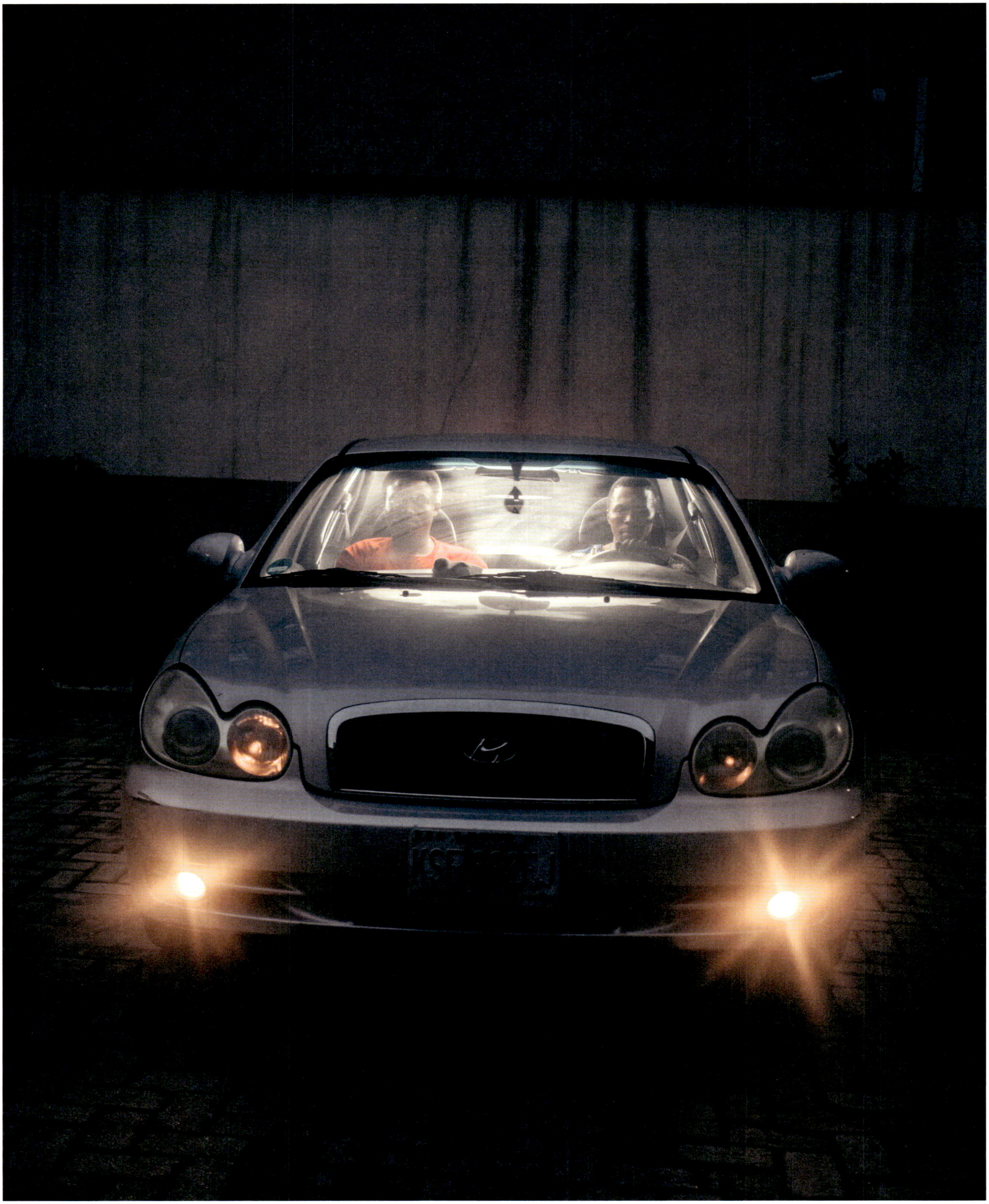

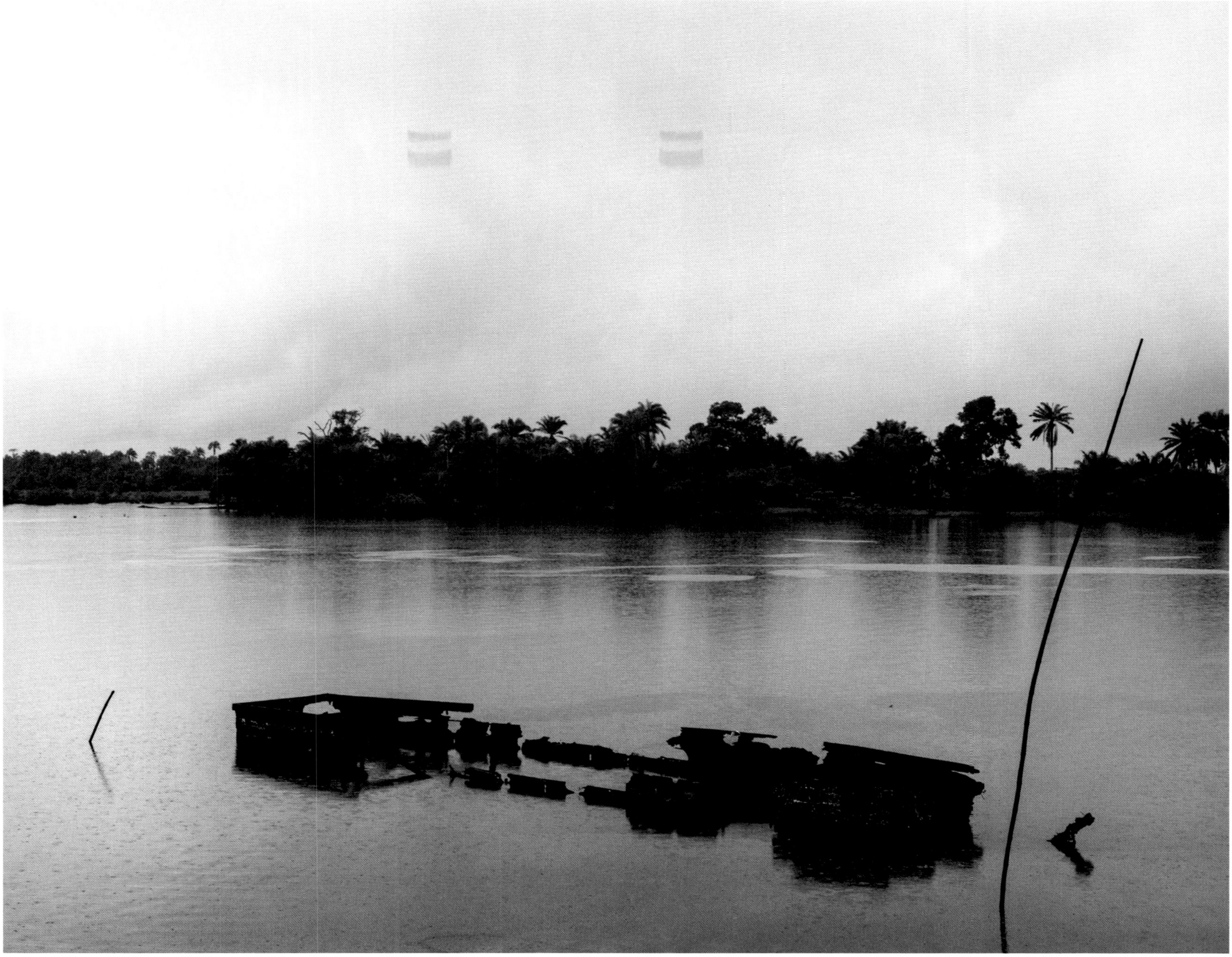

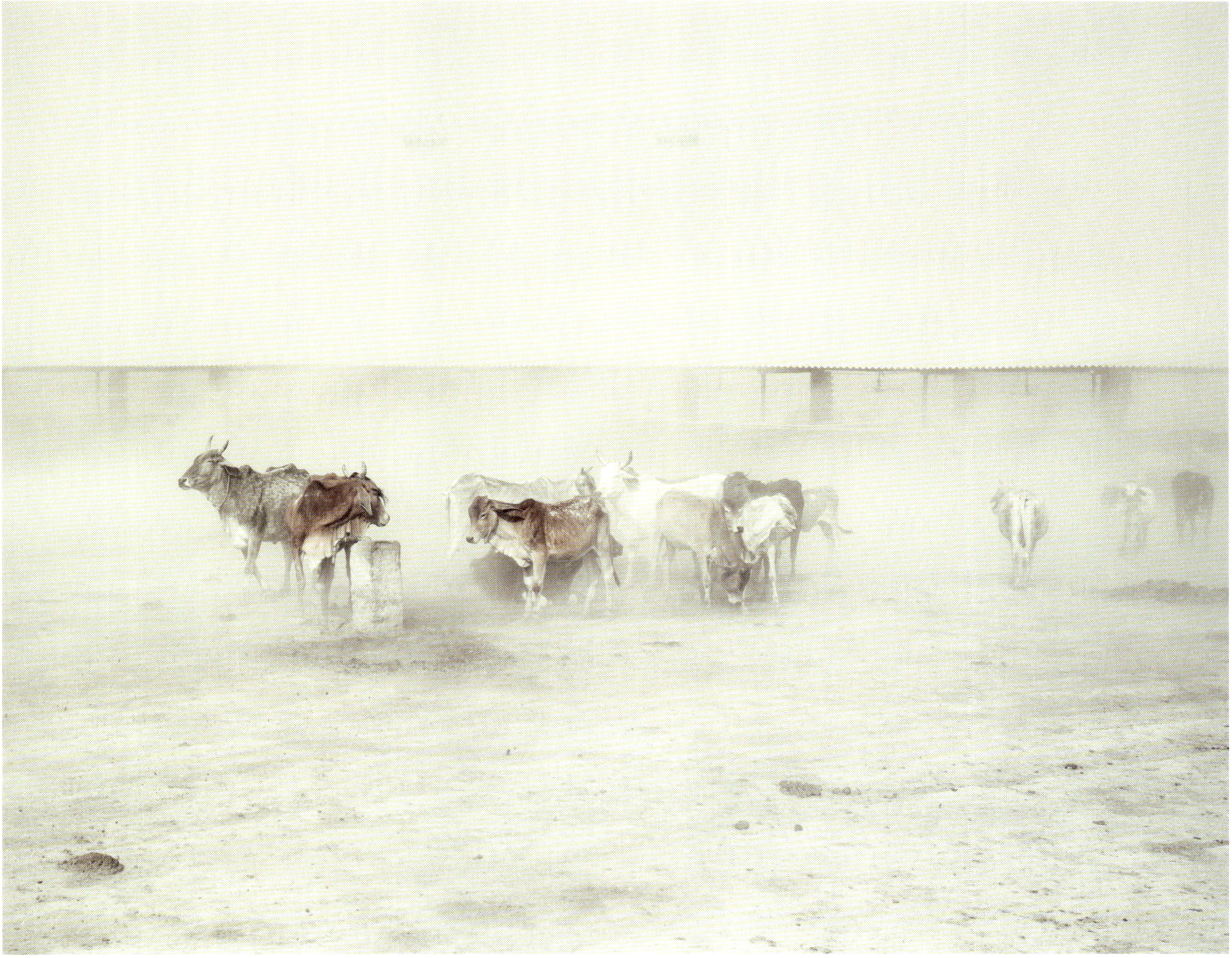

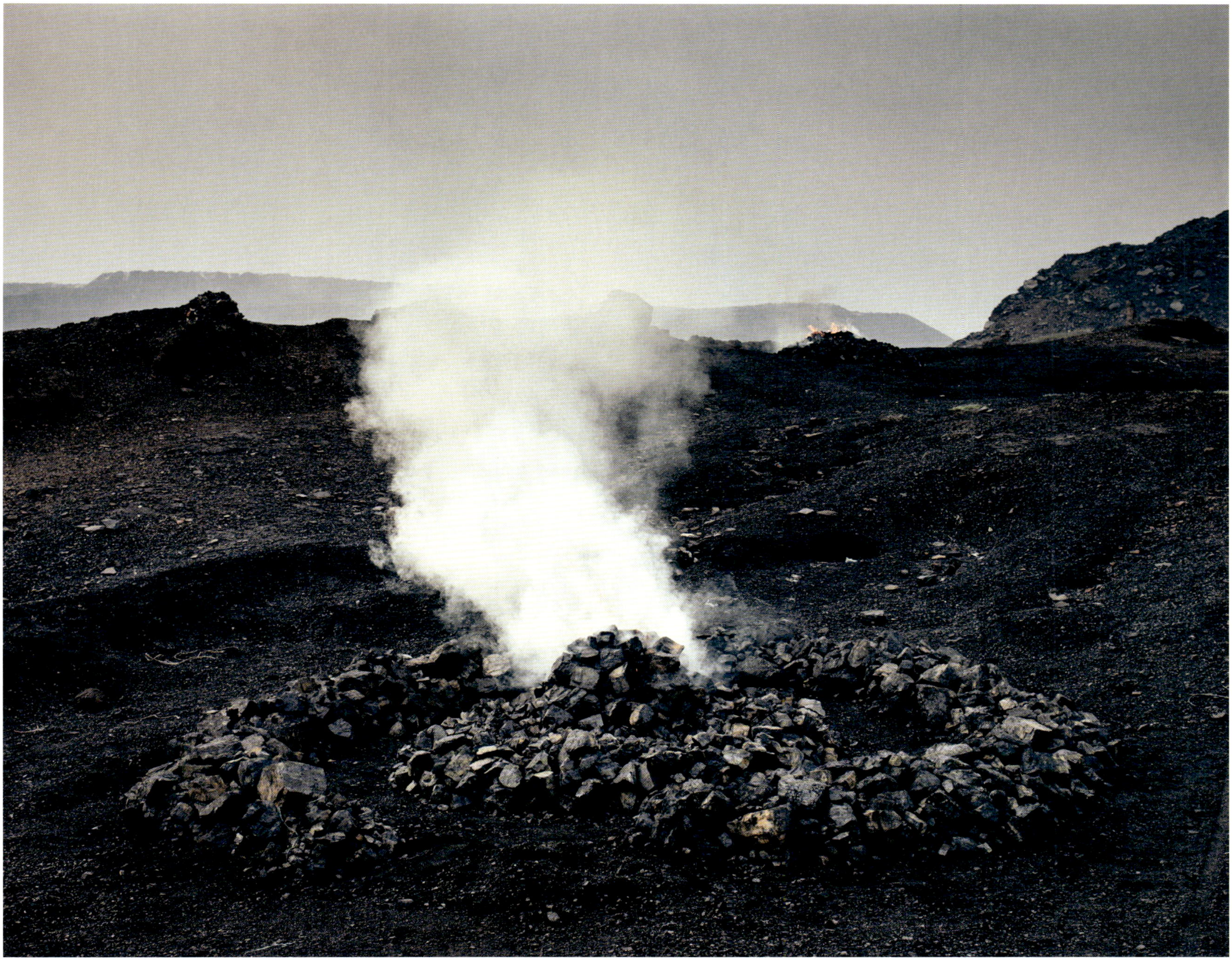

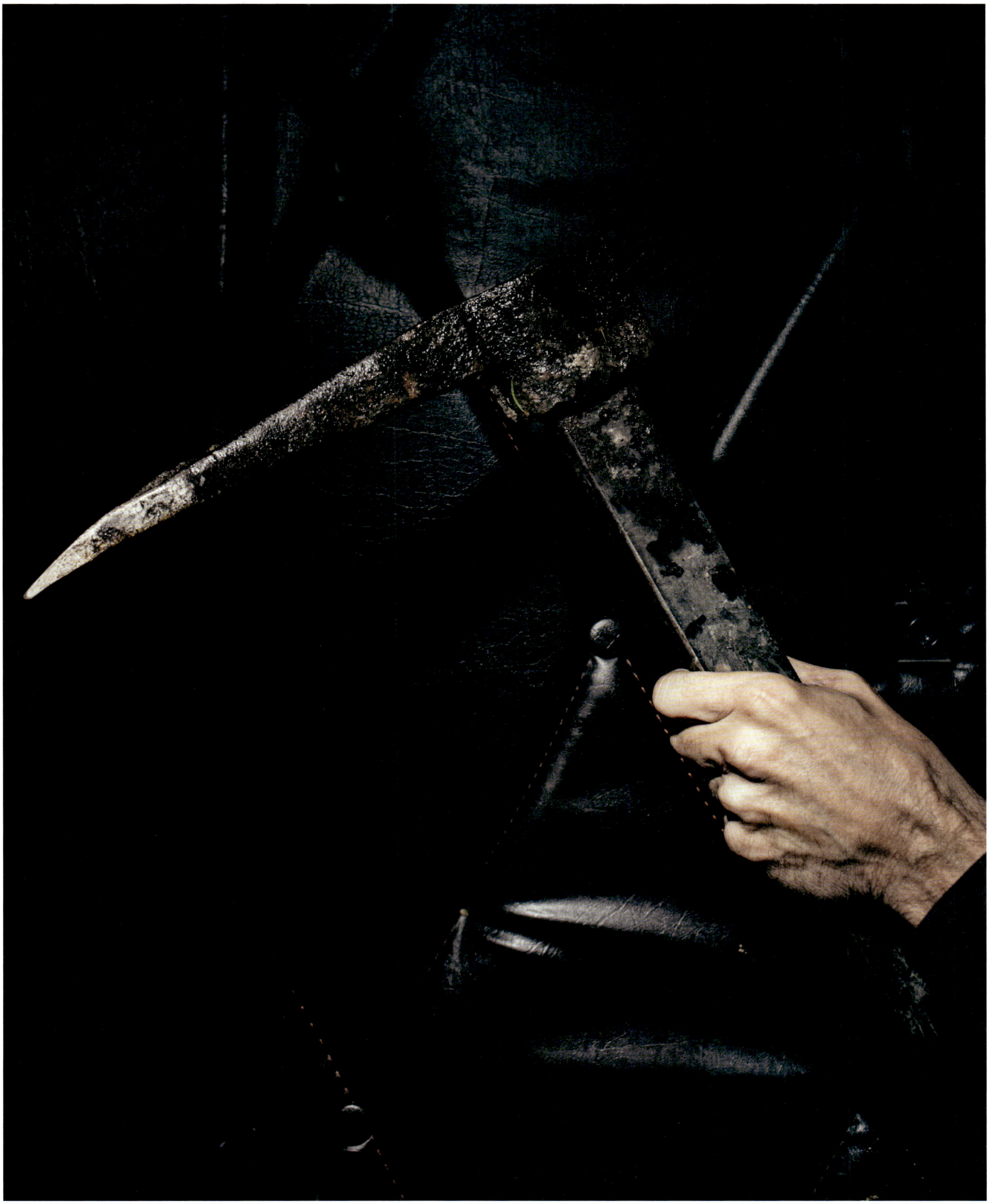

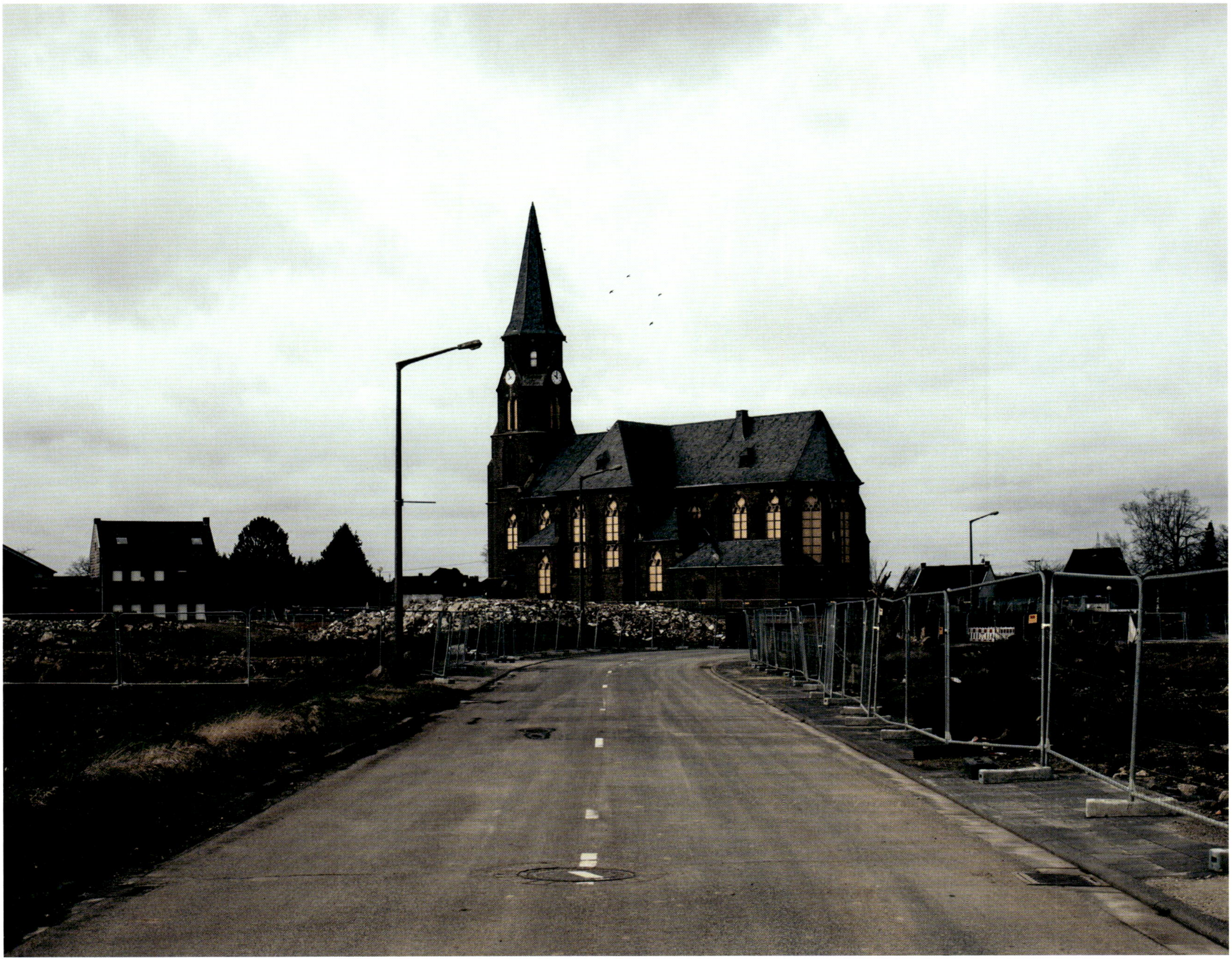

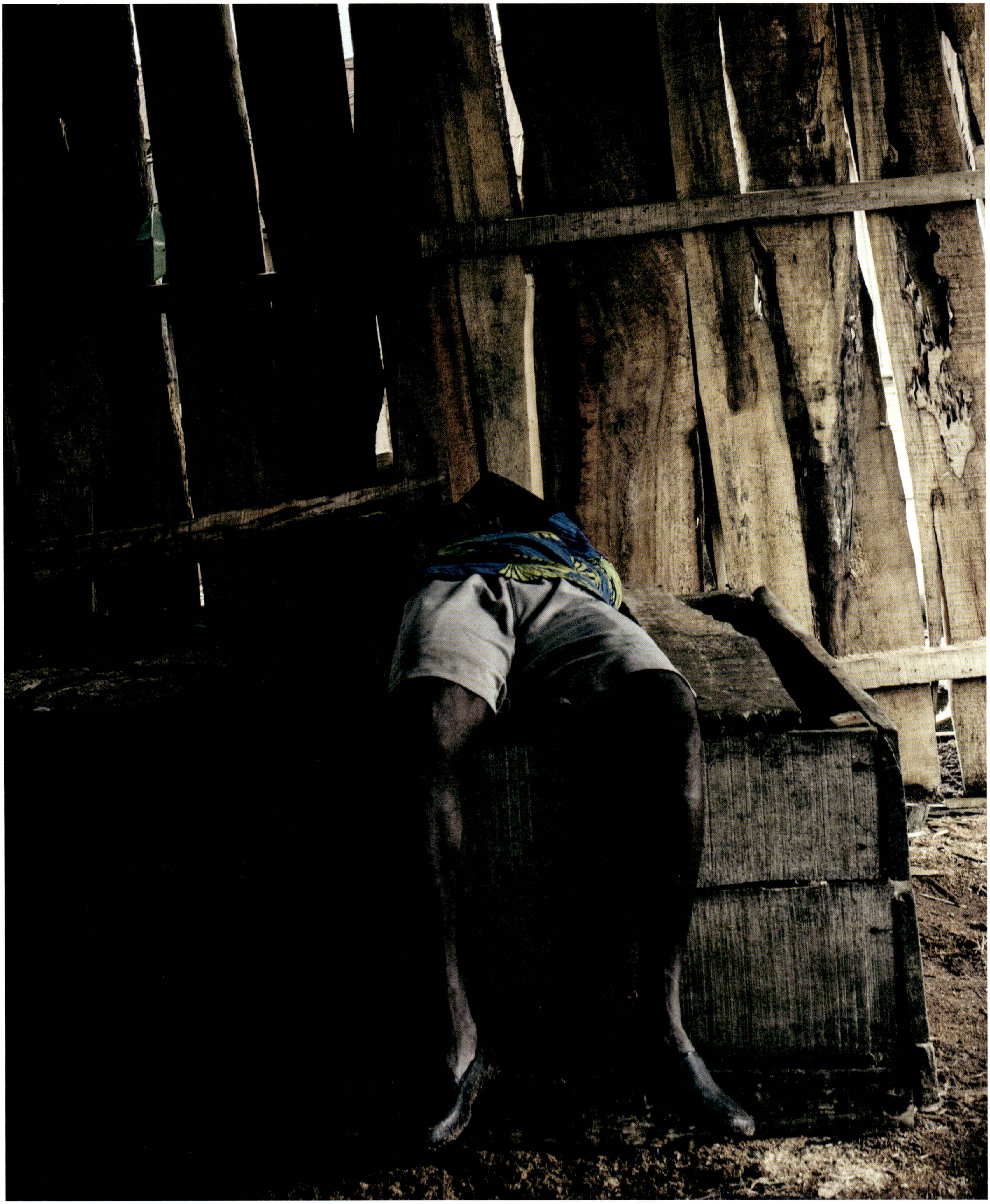

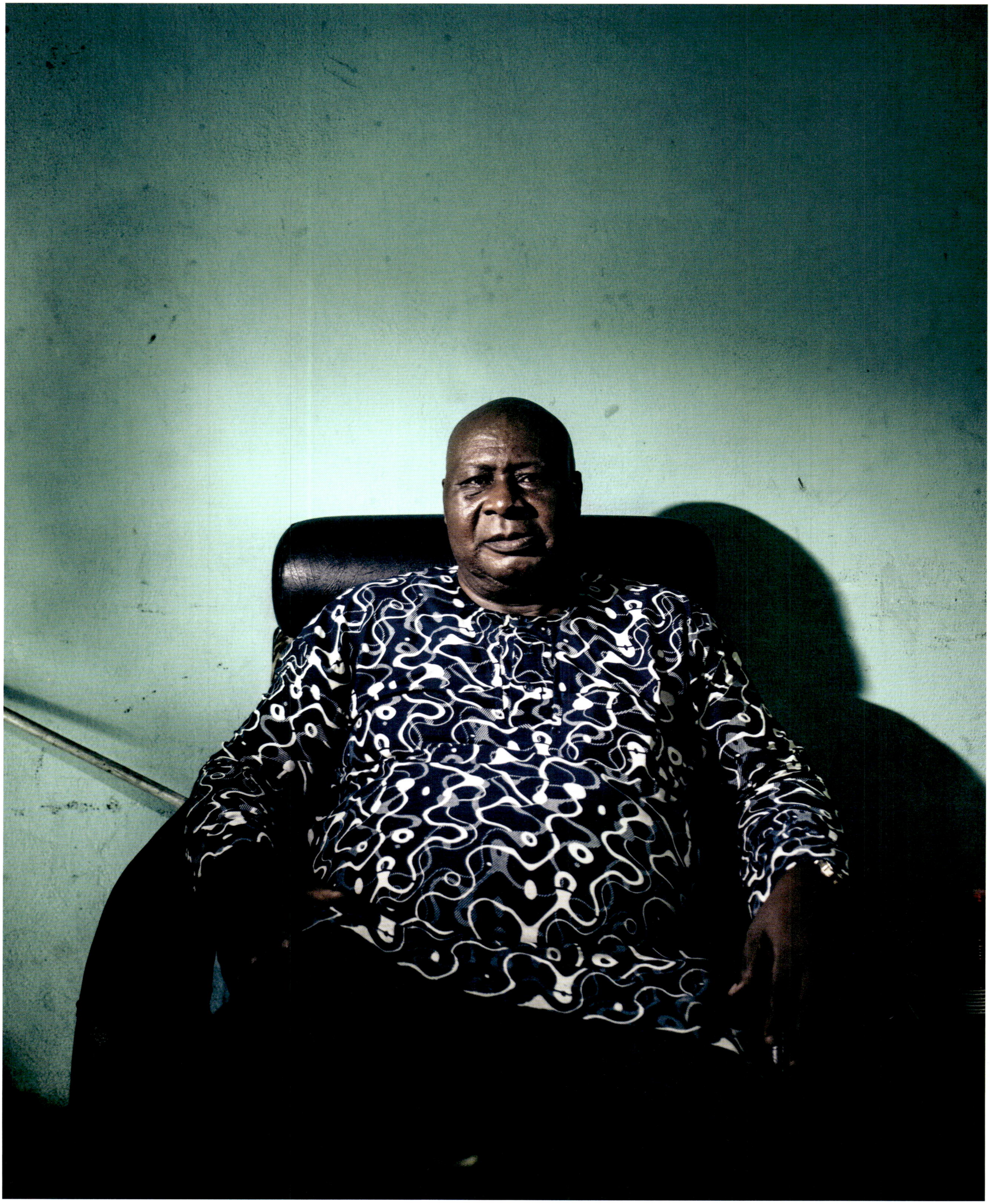

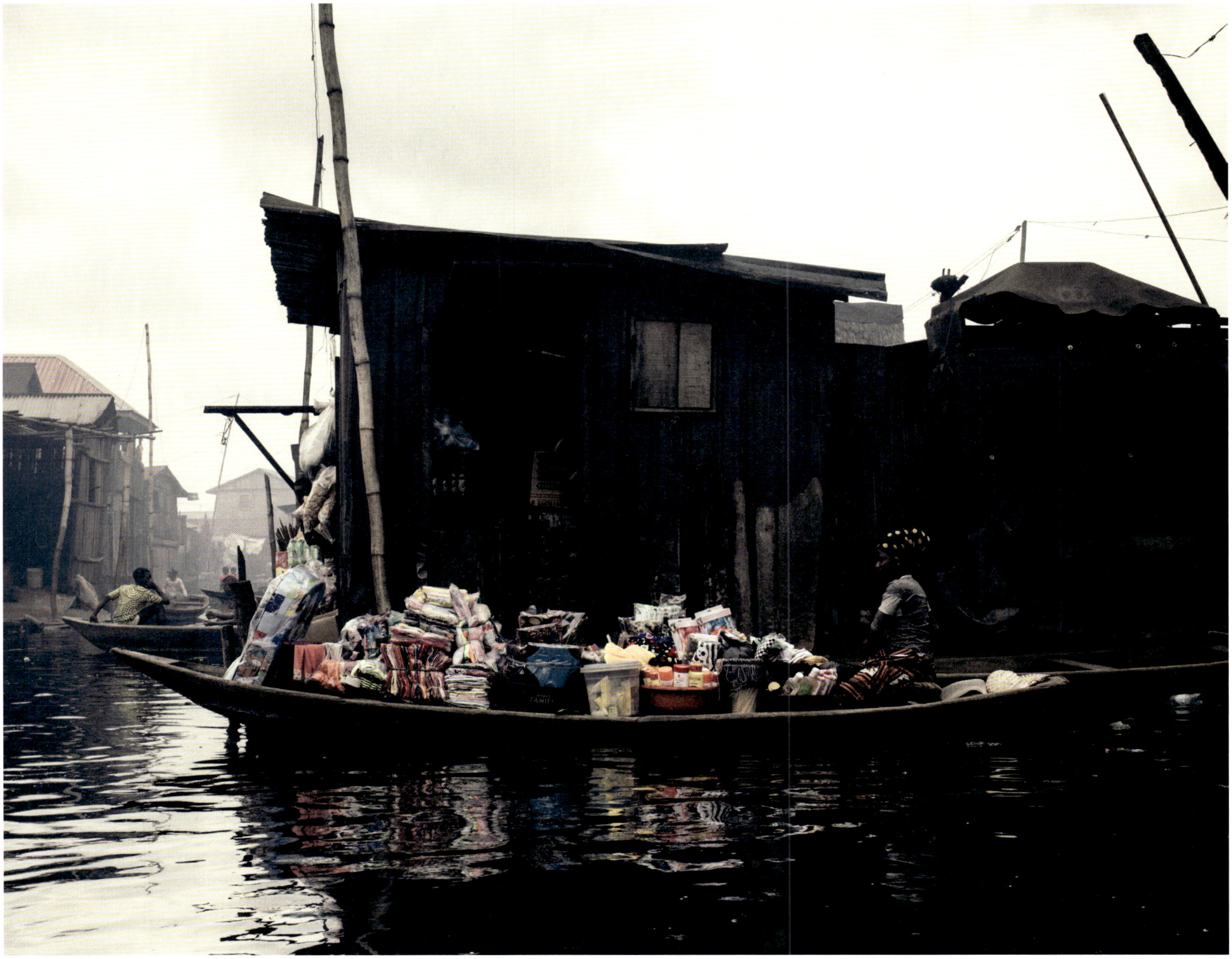

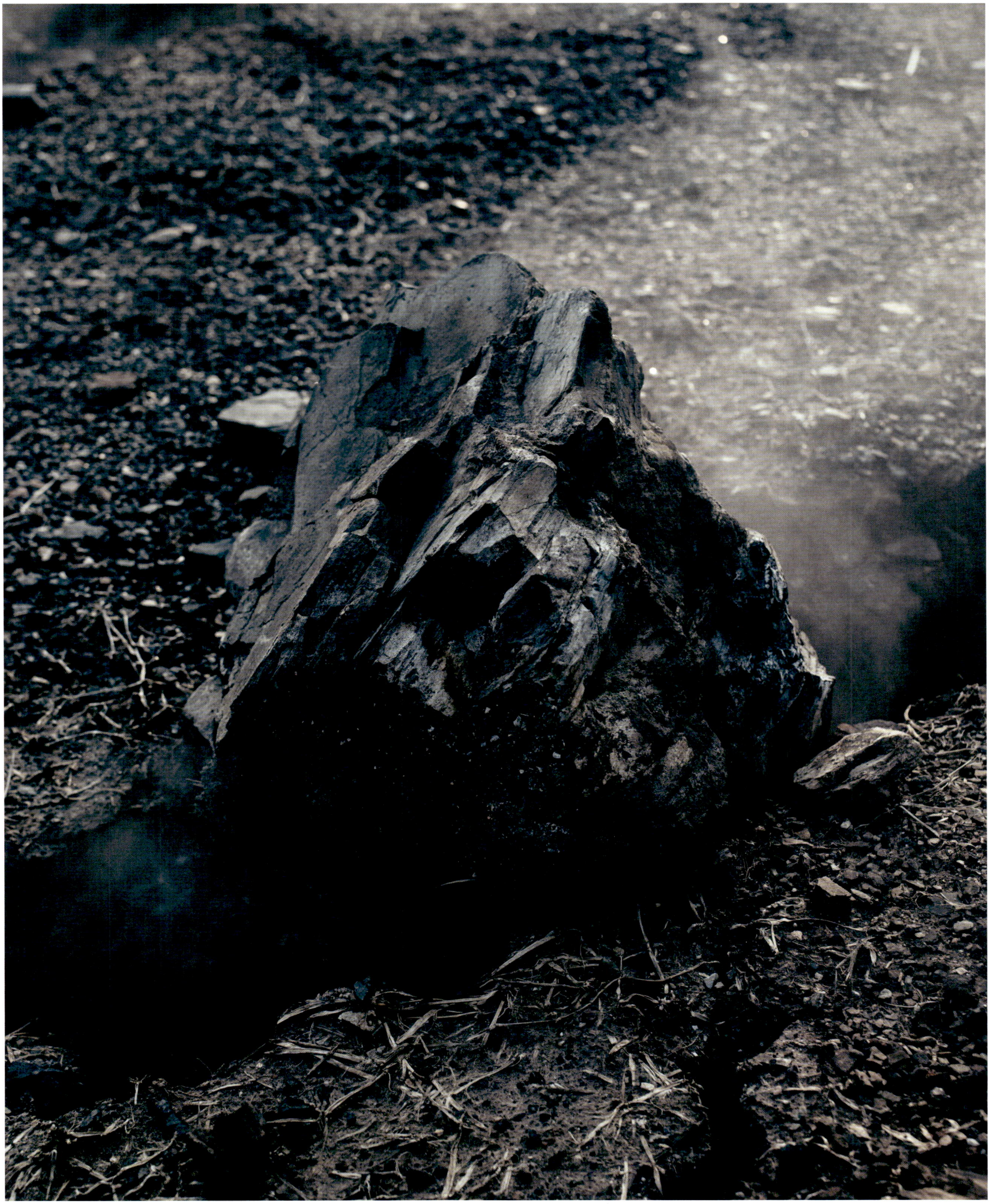

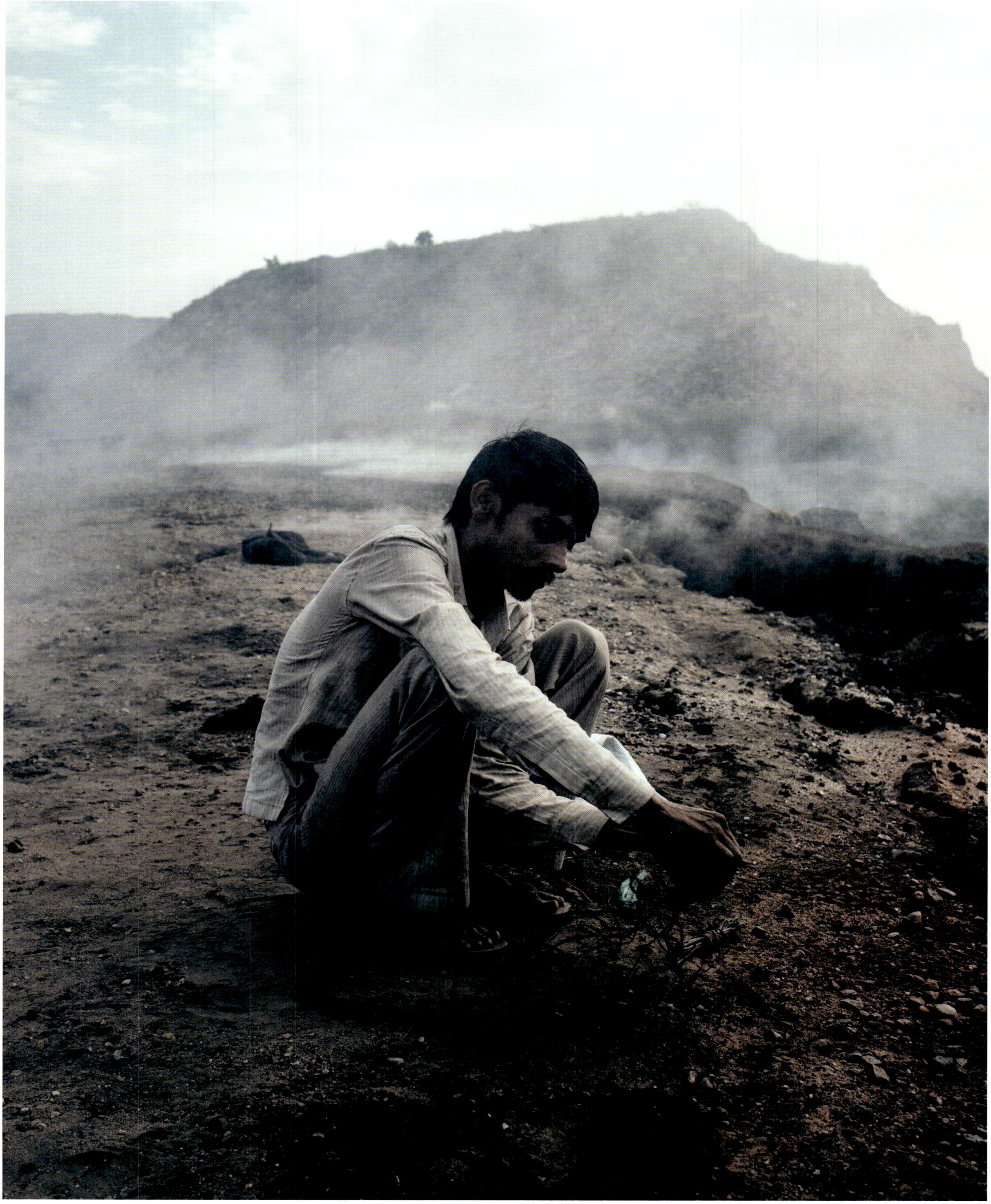

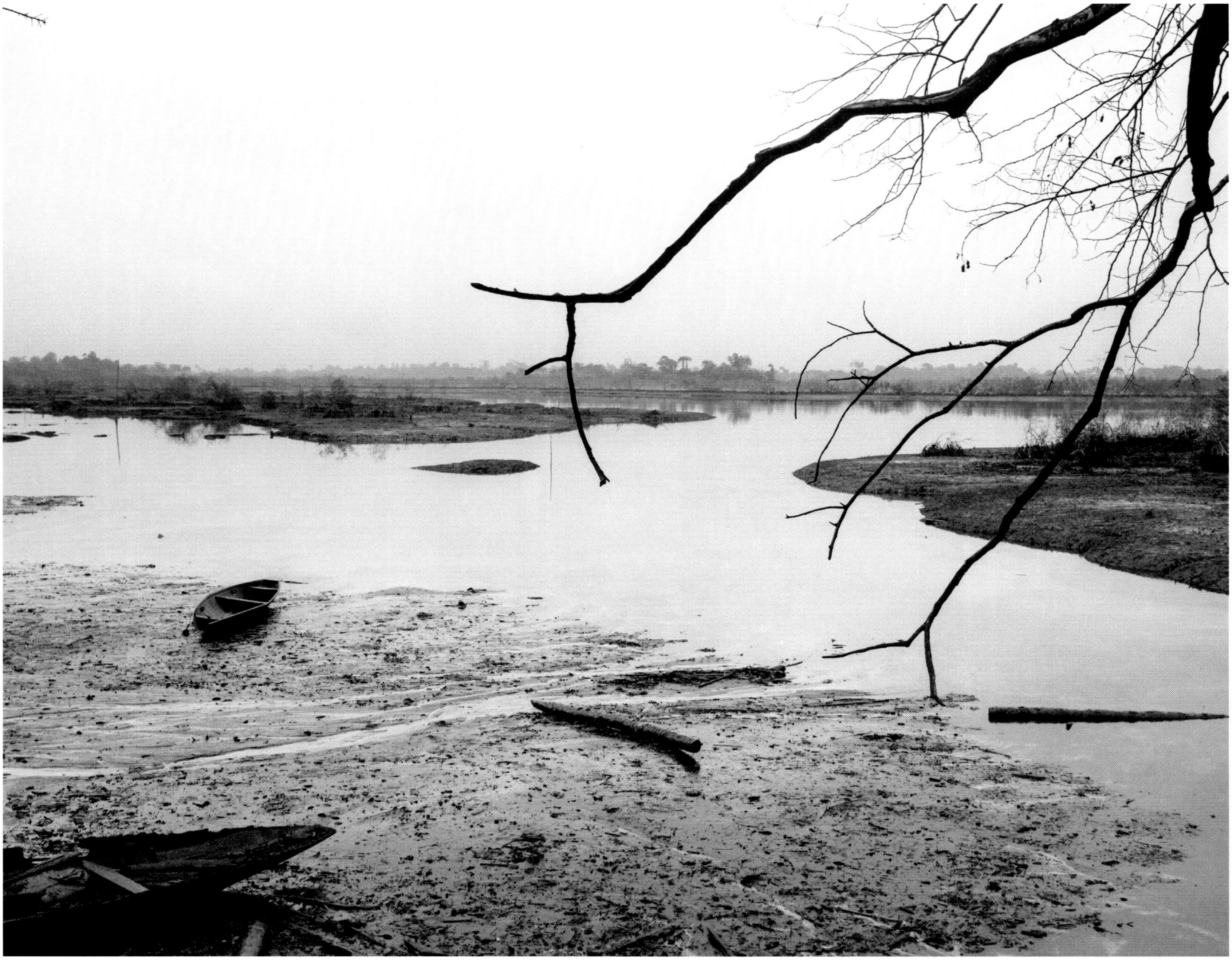

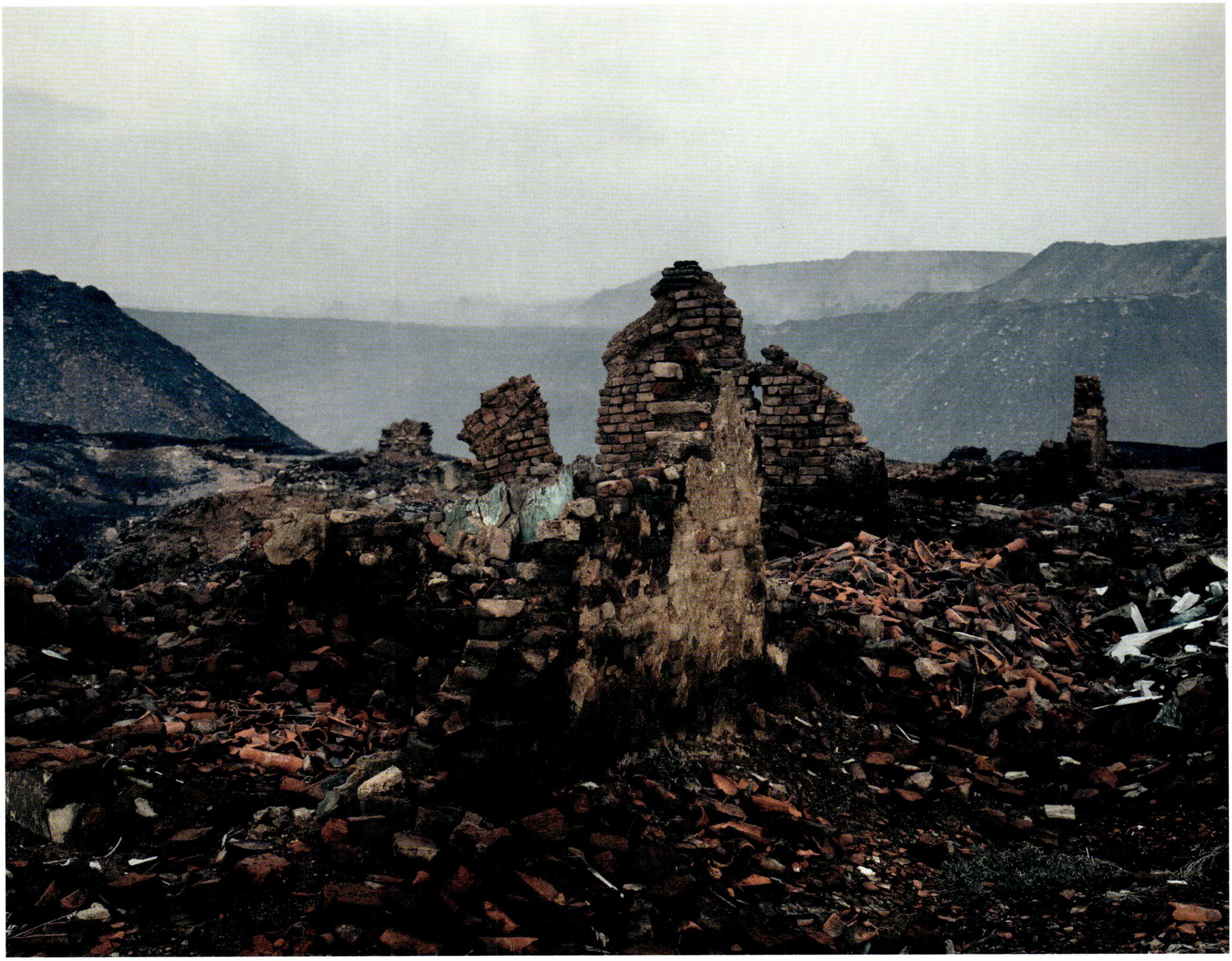

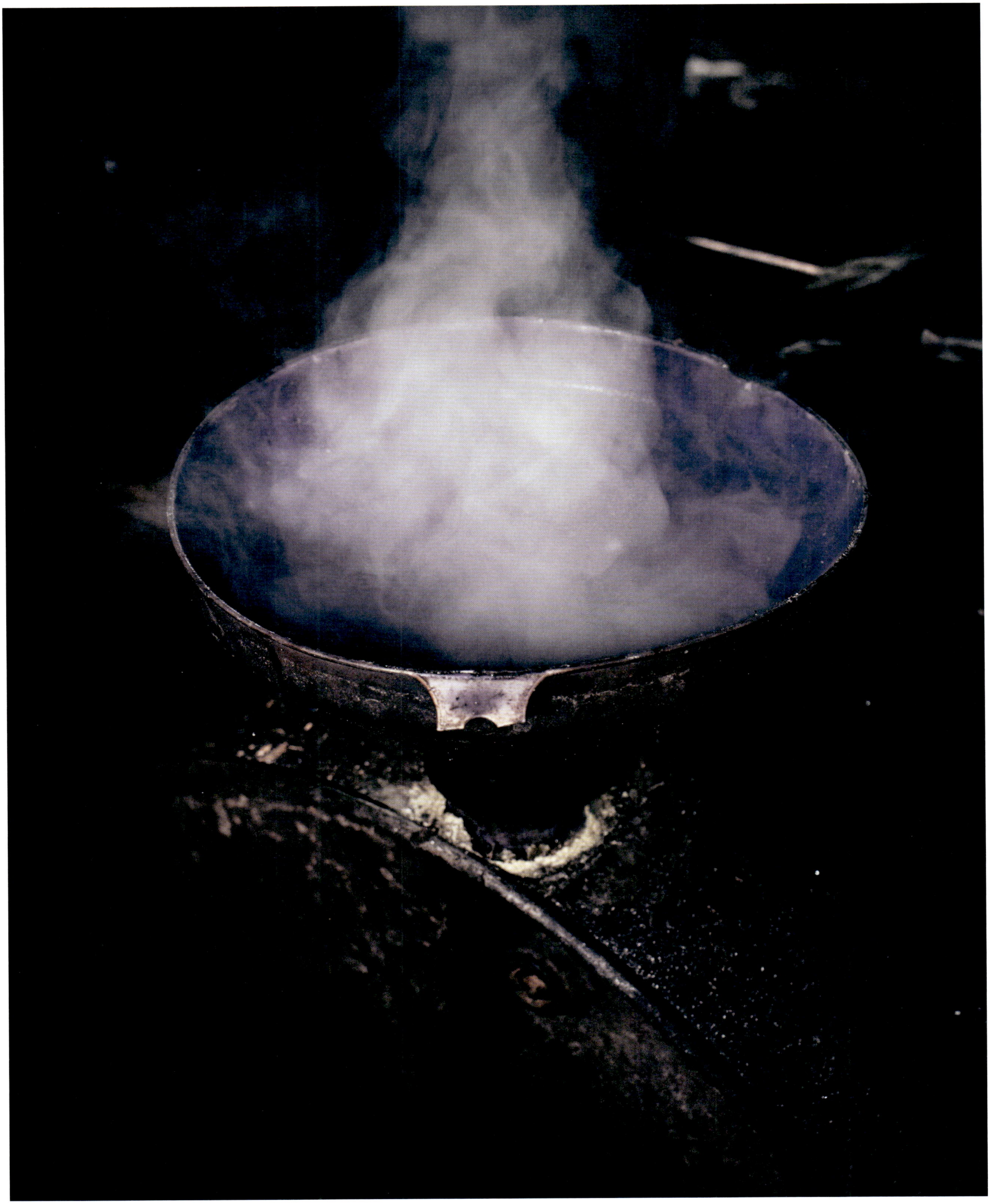

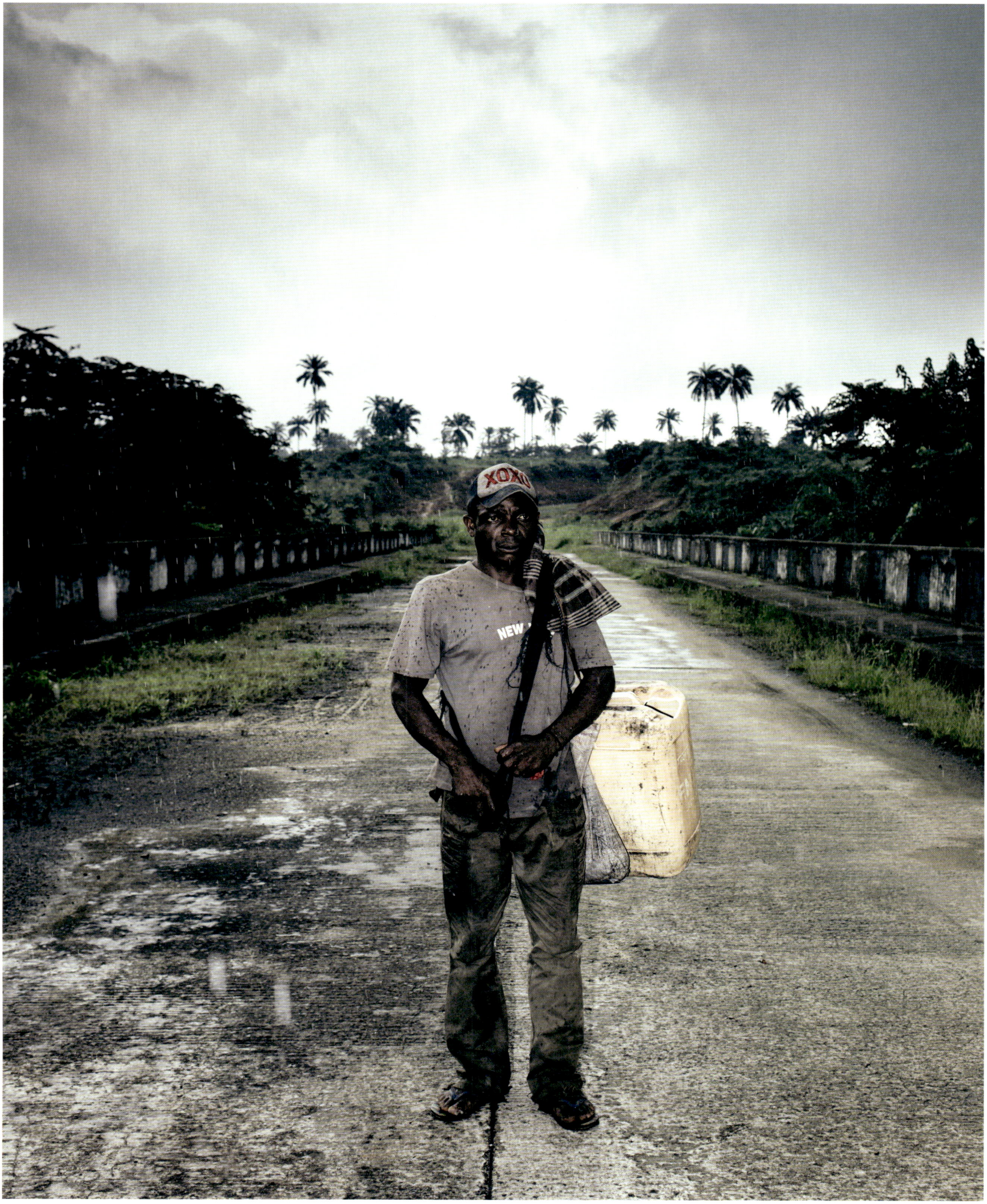
XOXO
NEW

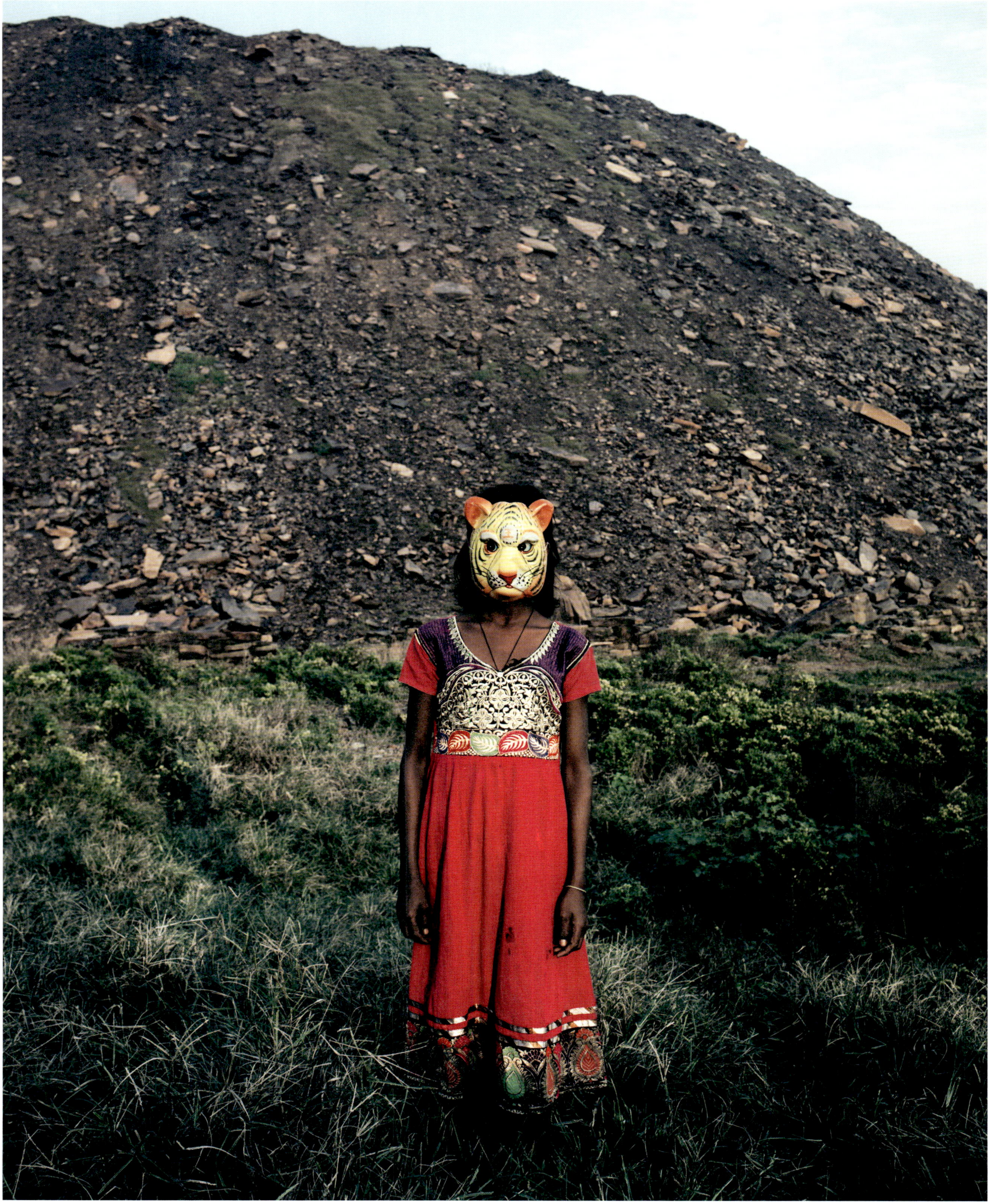

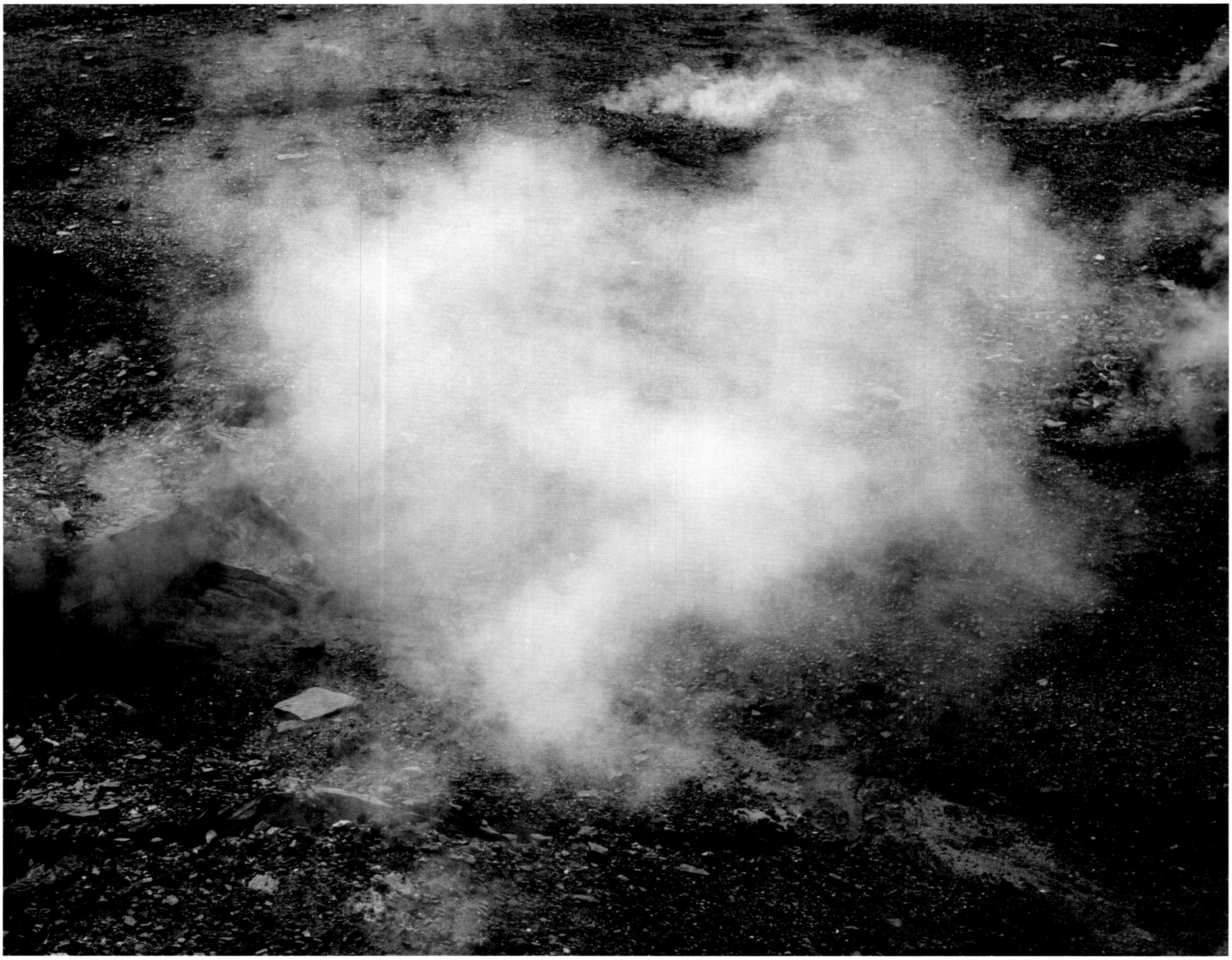

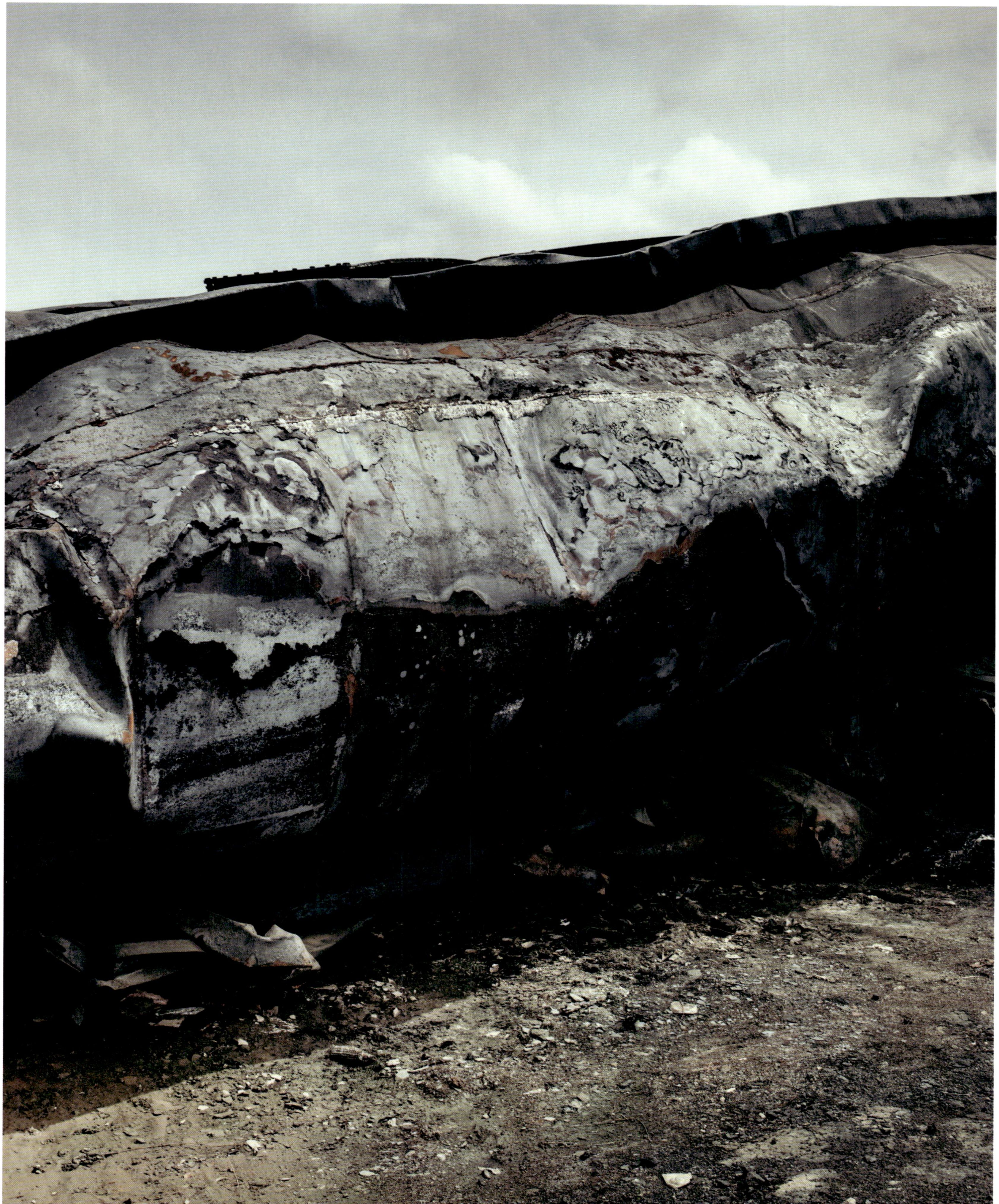

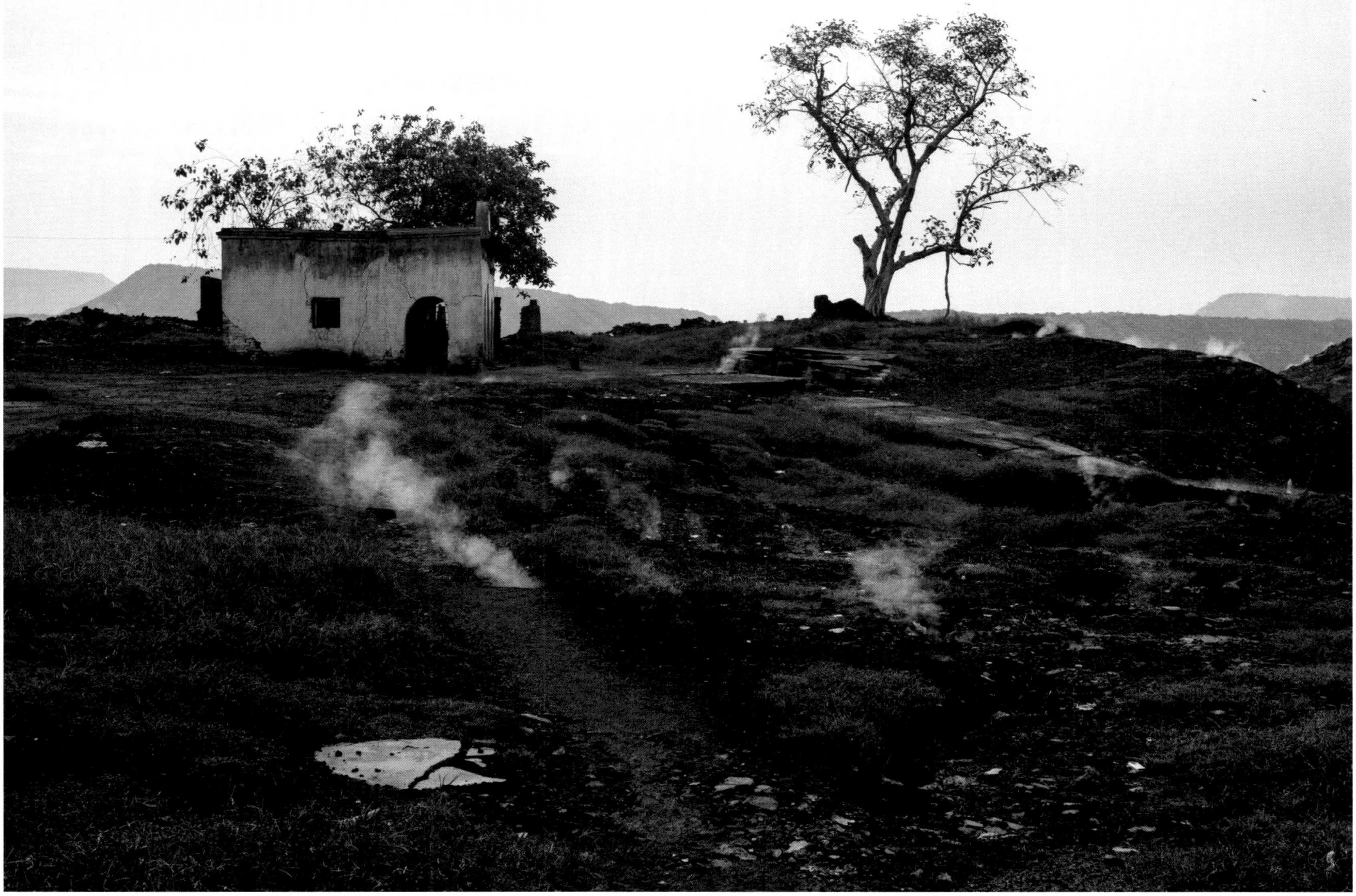

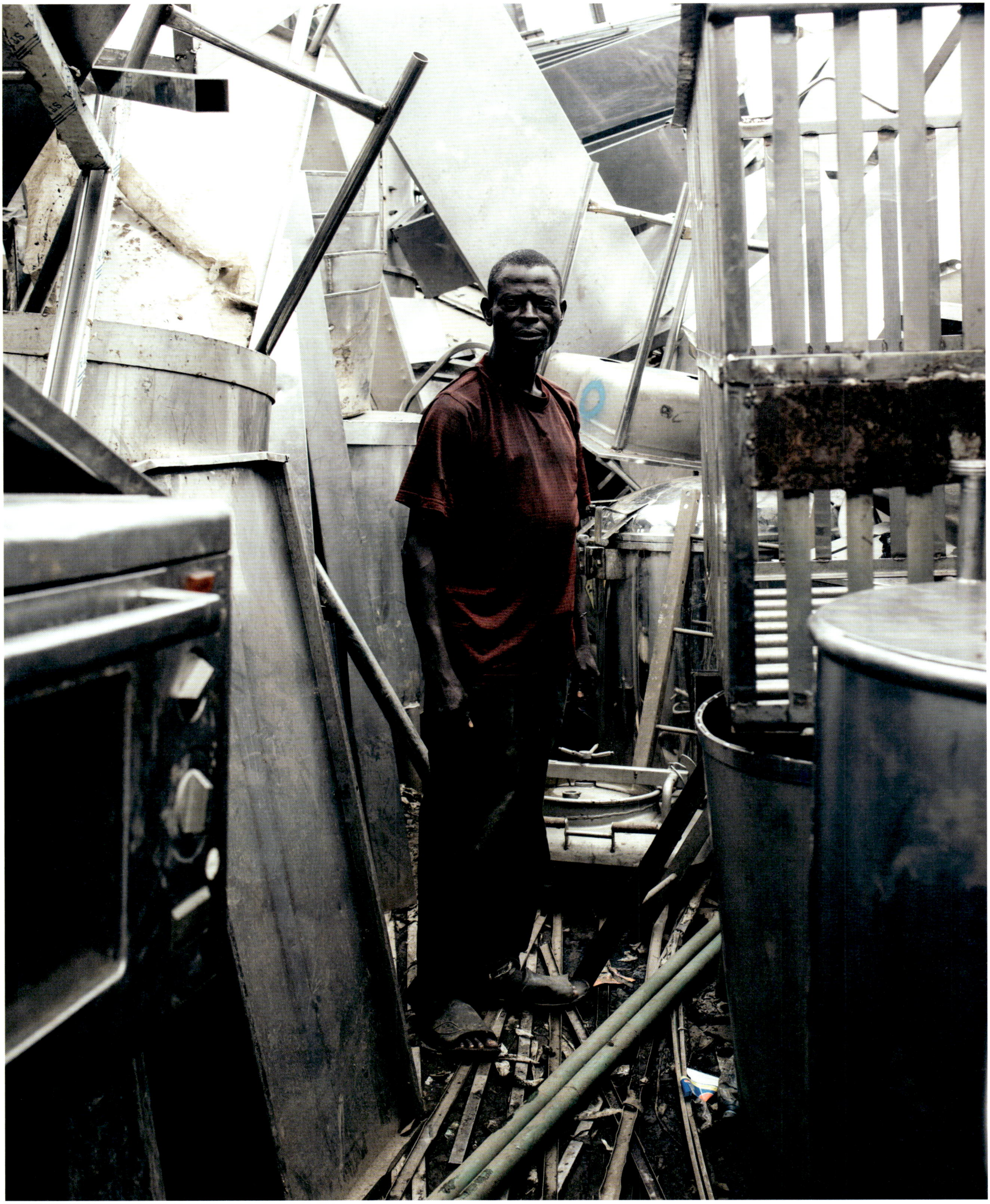

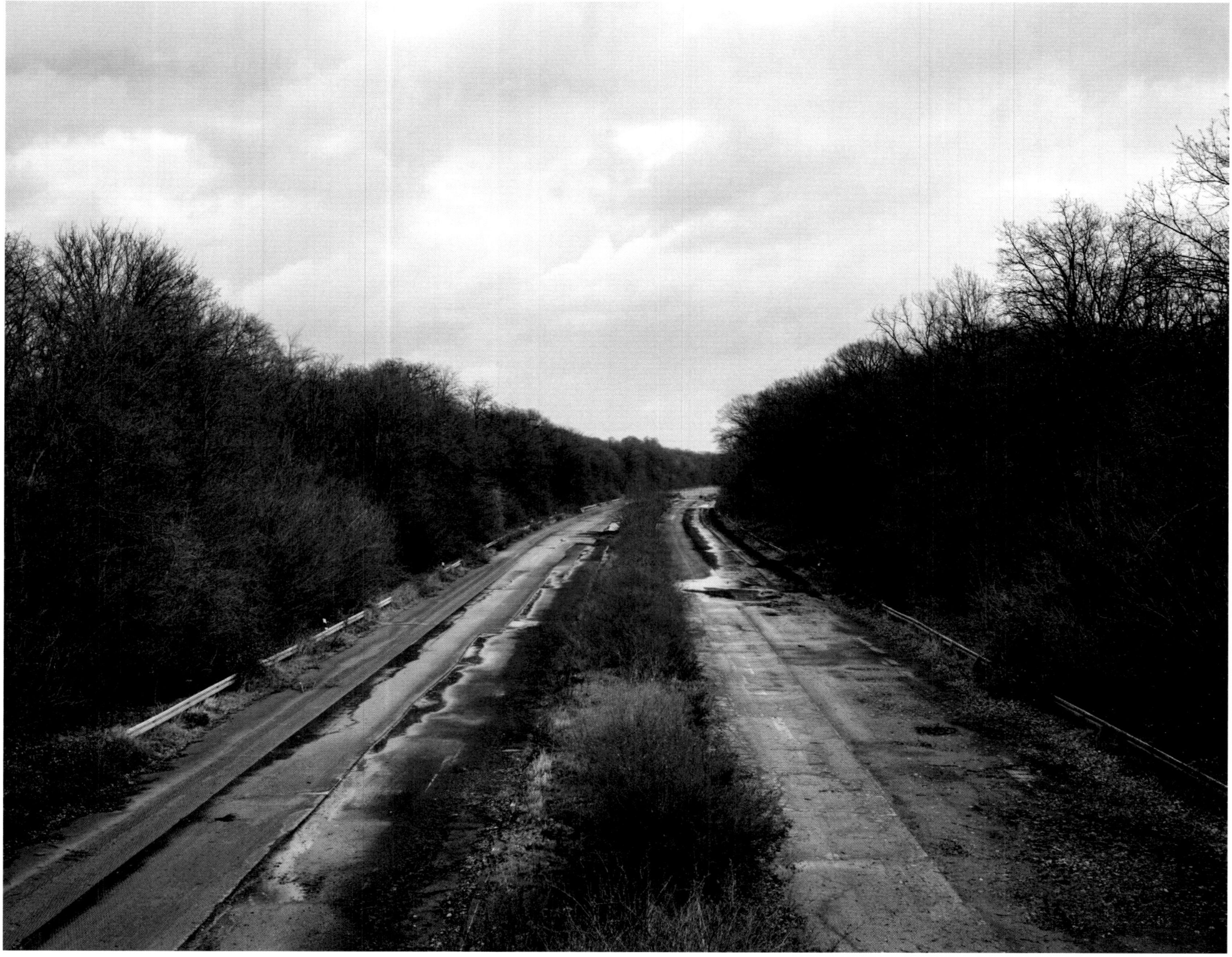

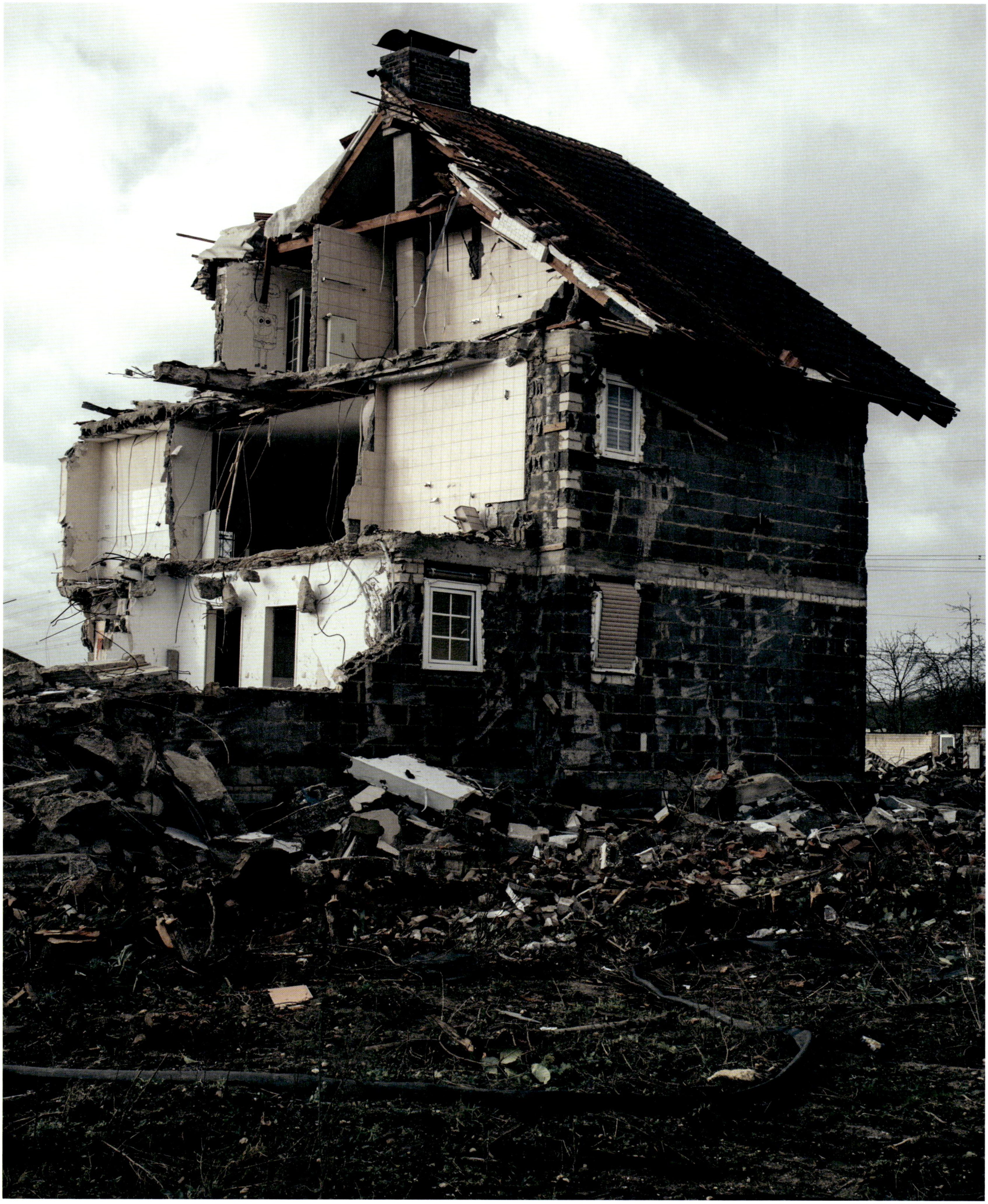

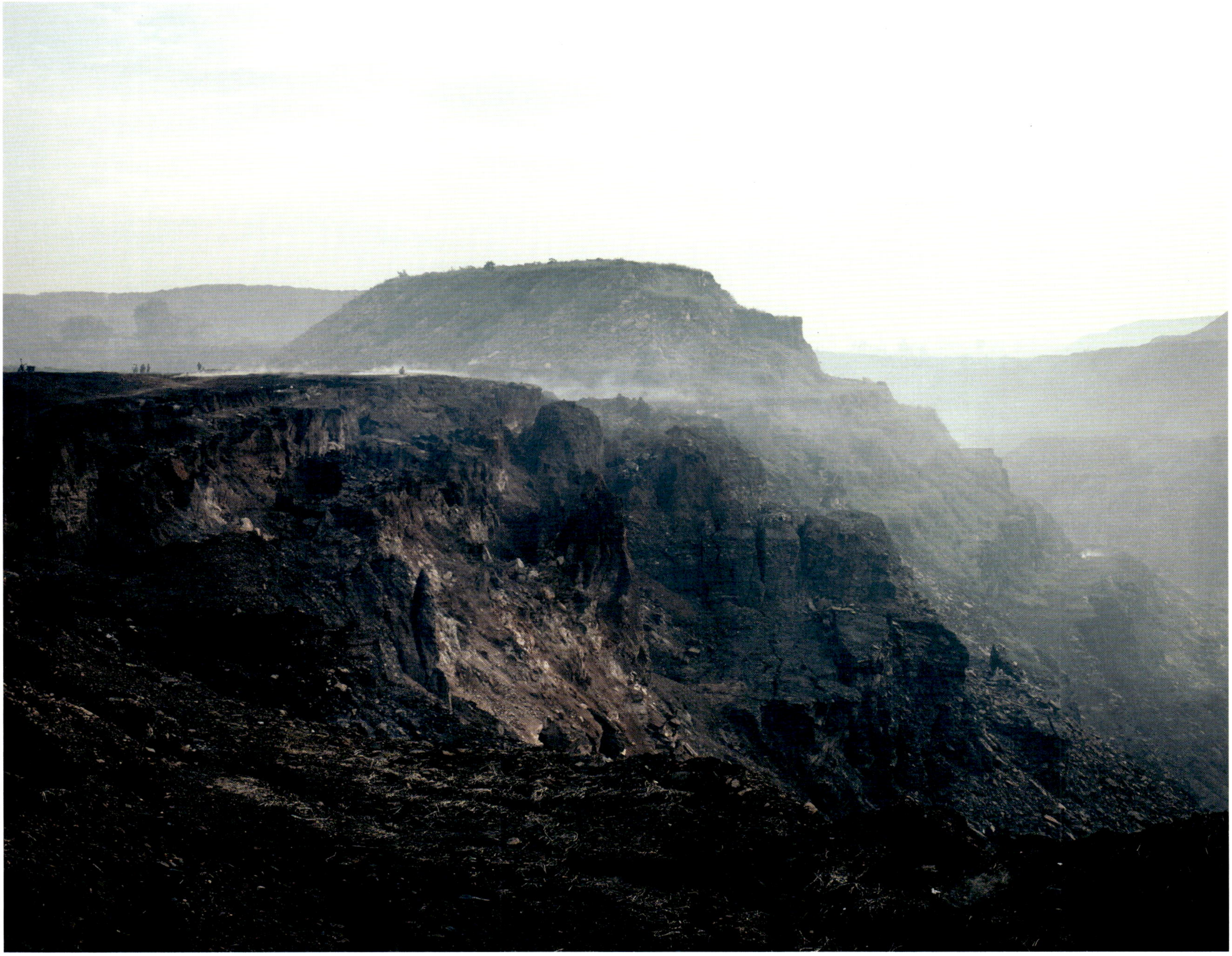

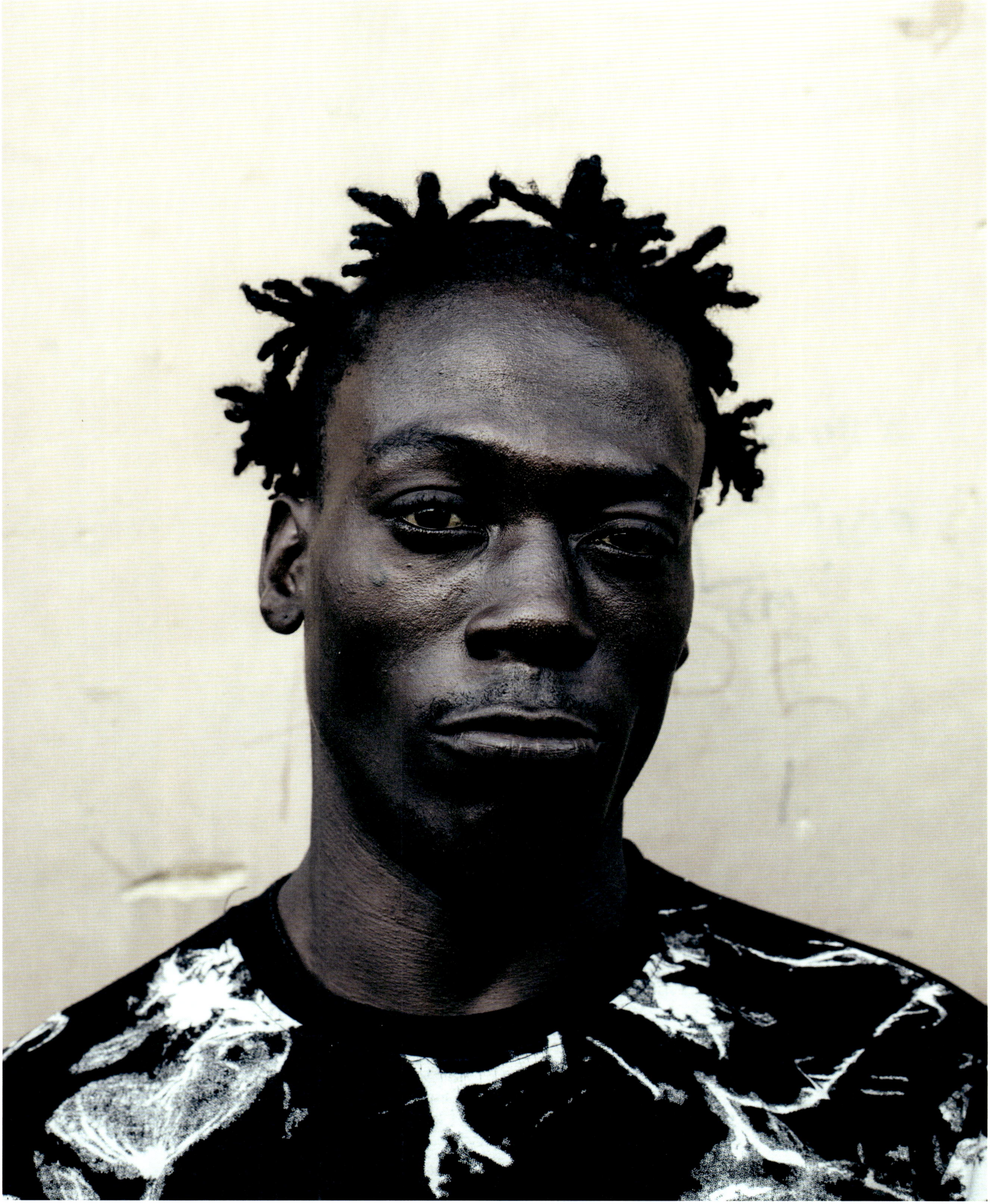

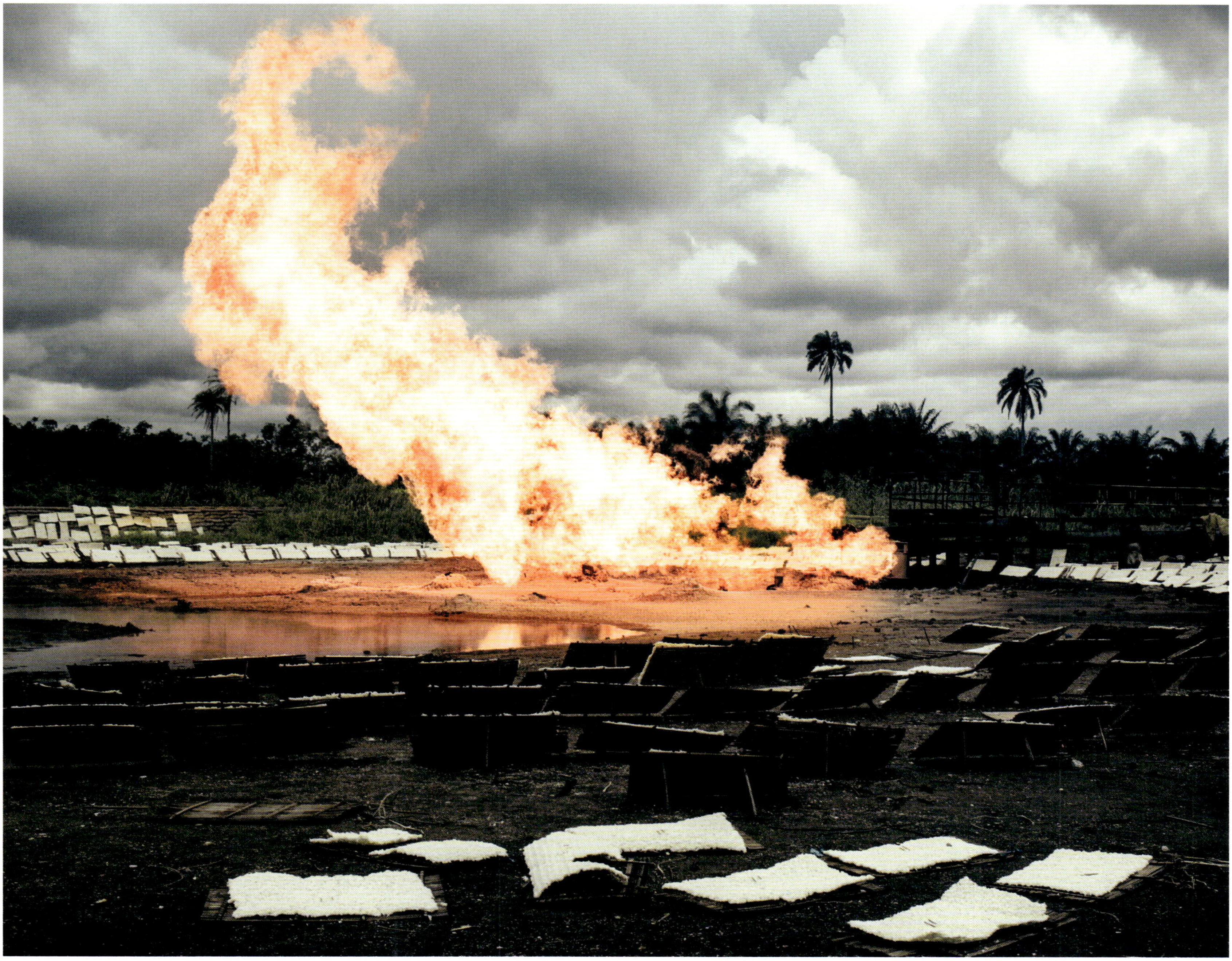

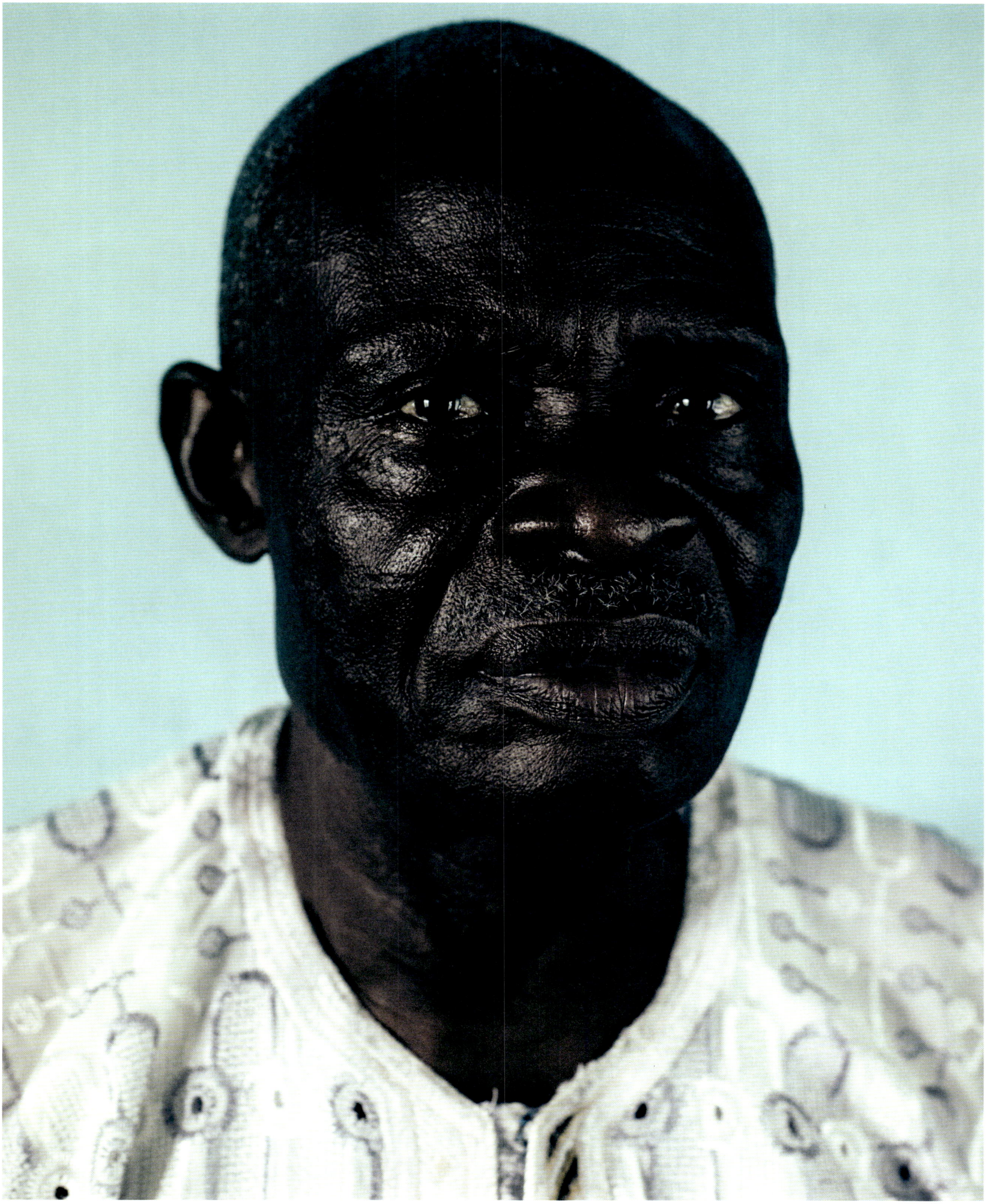

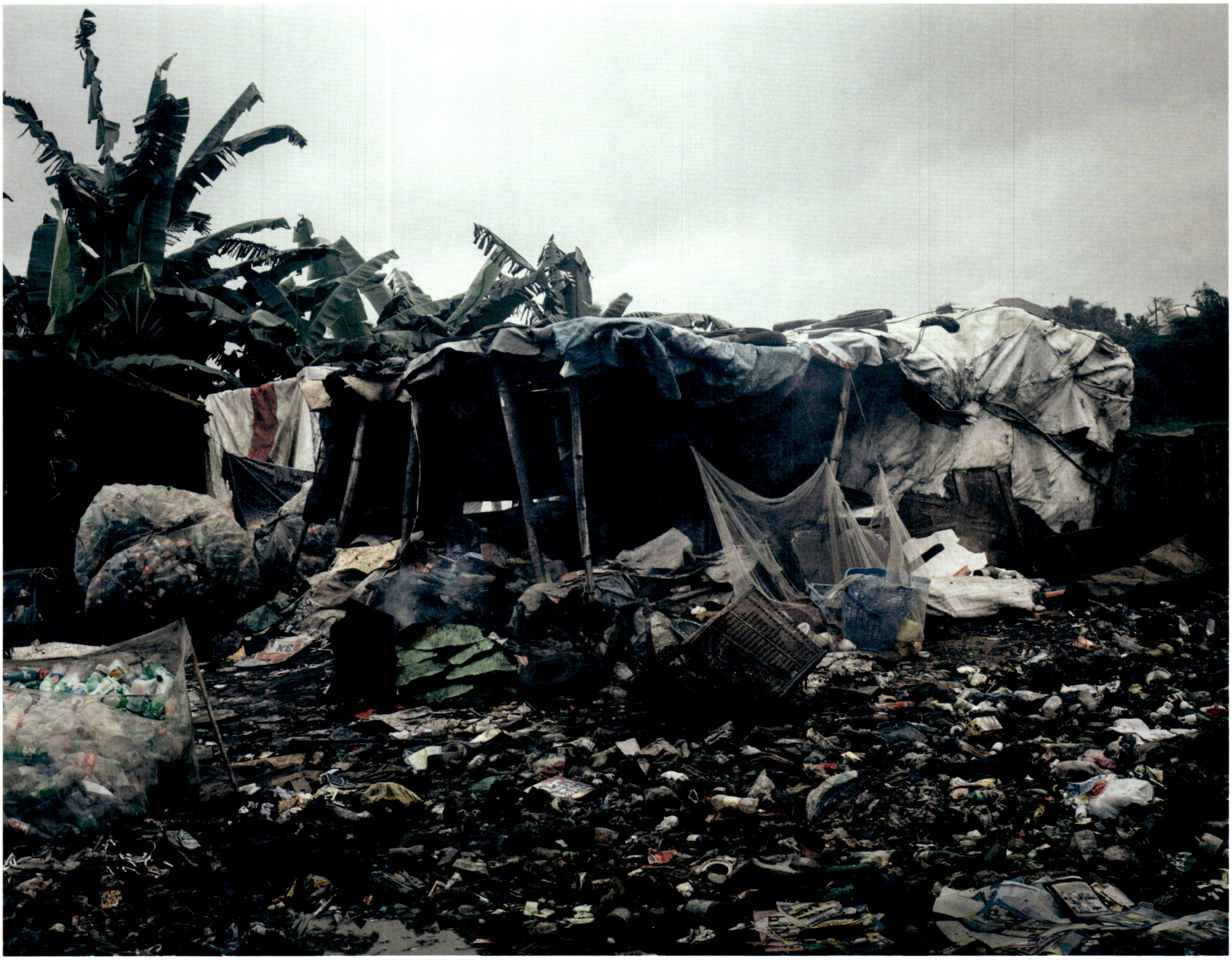

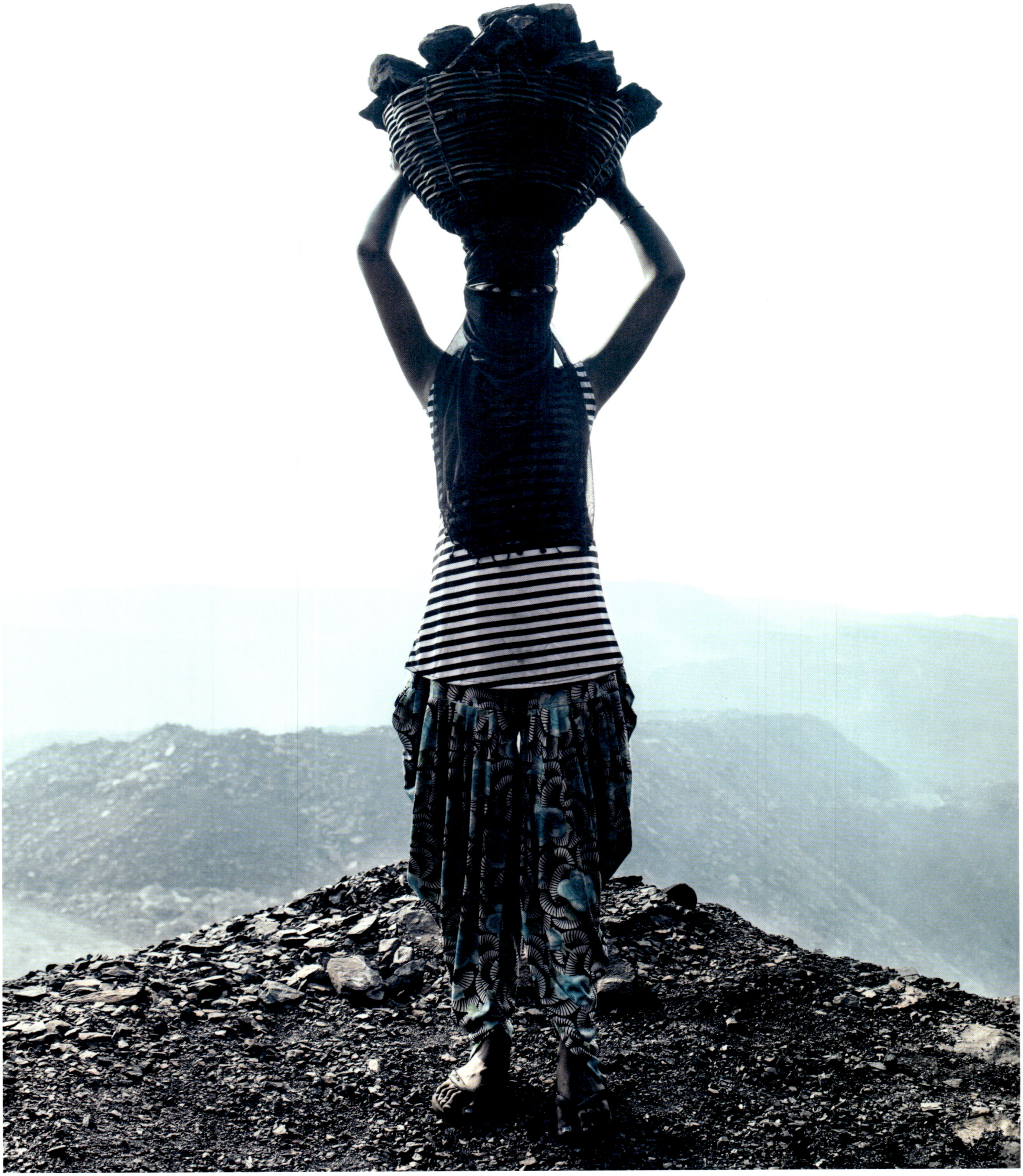

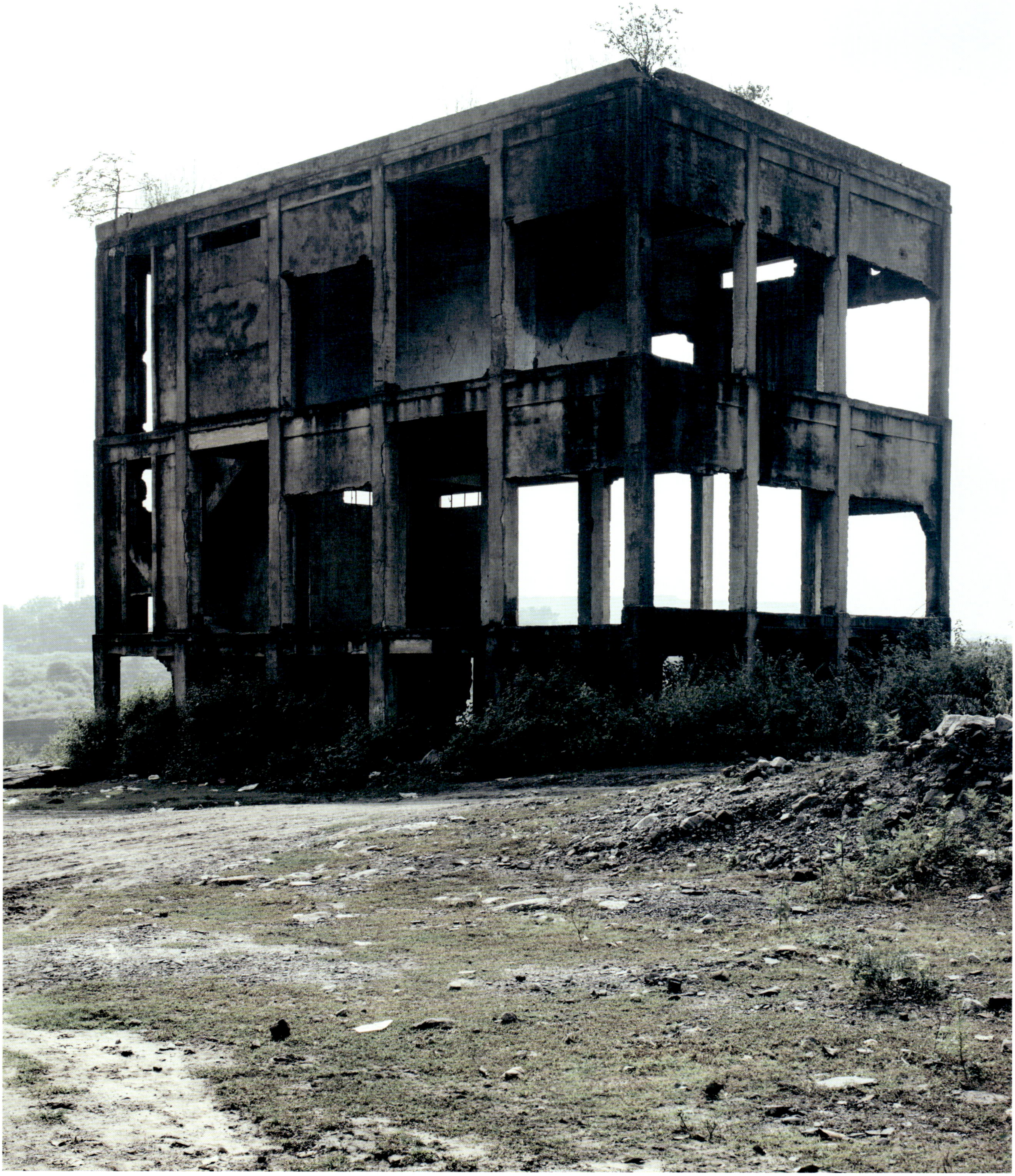

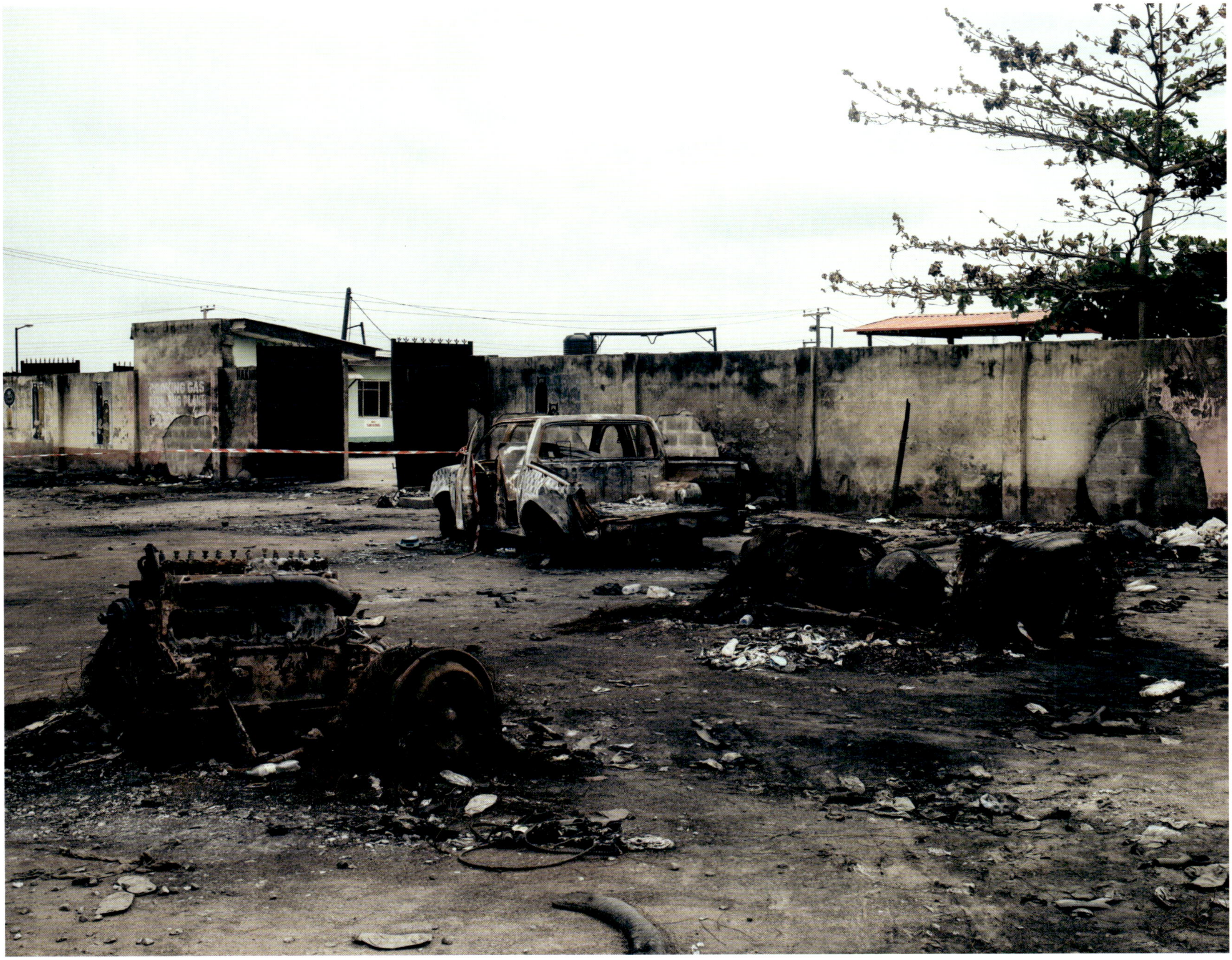

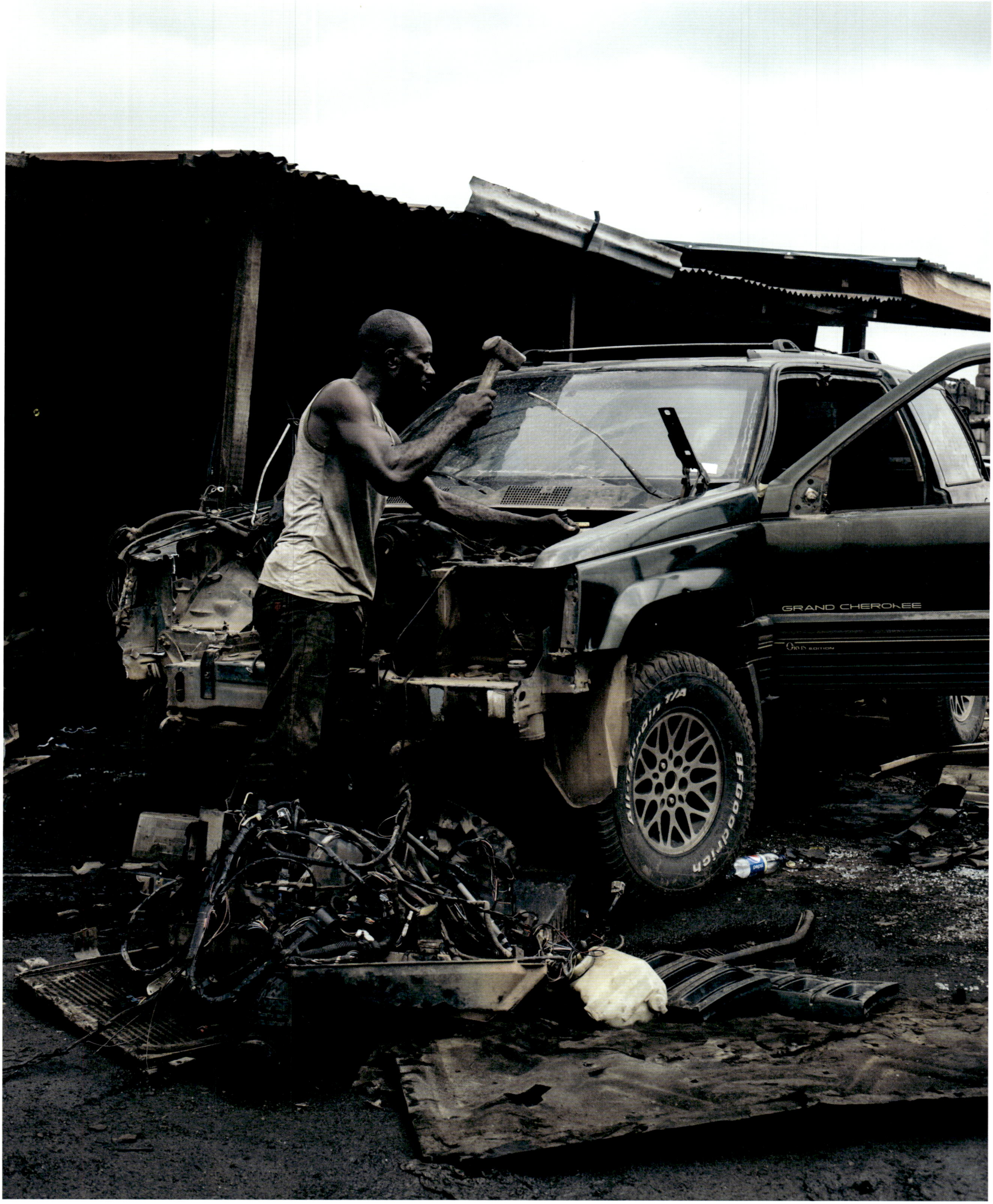
GRAND CHEROKEE
BFGoodrich

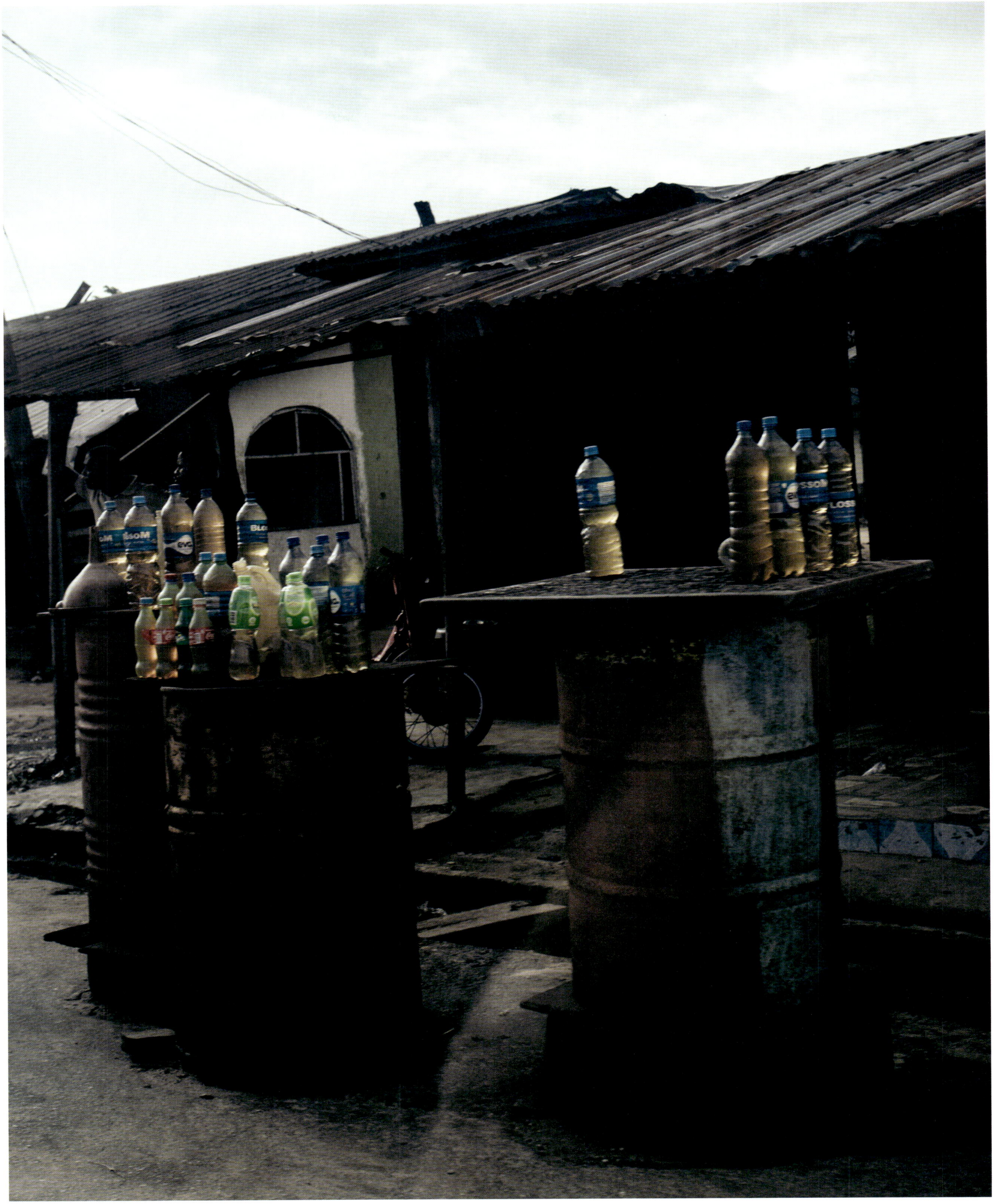

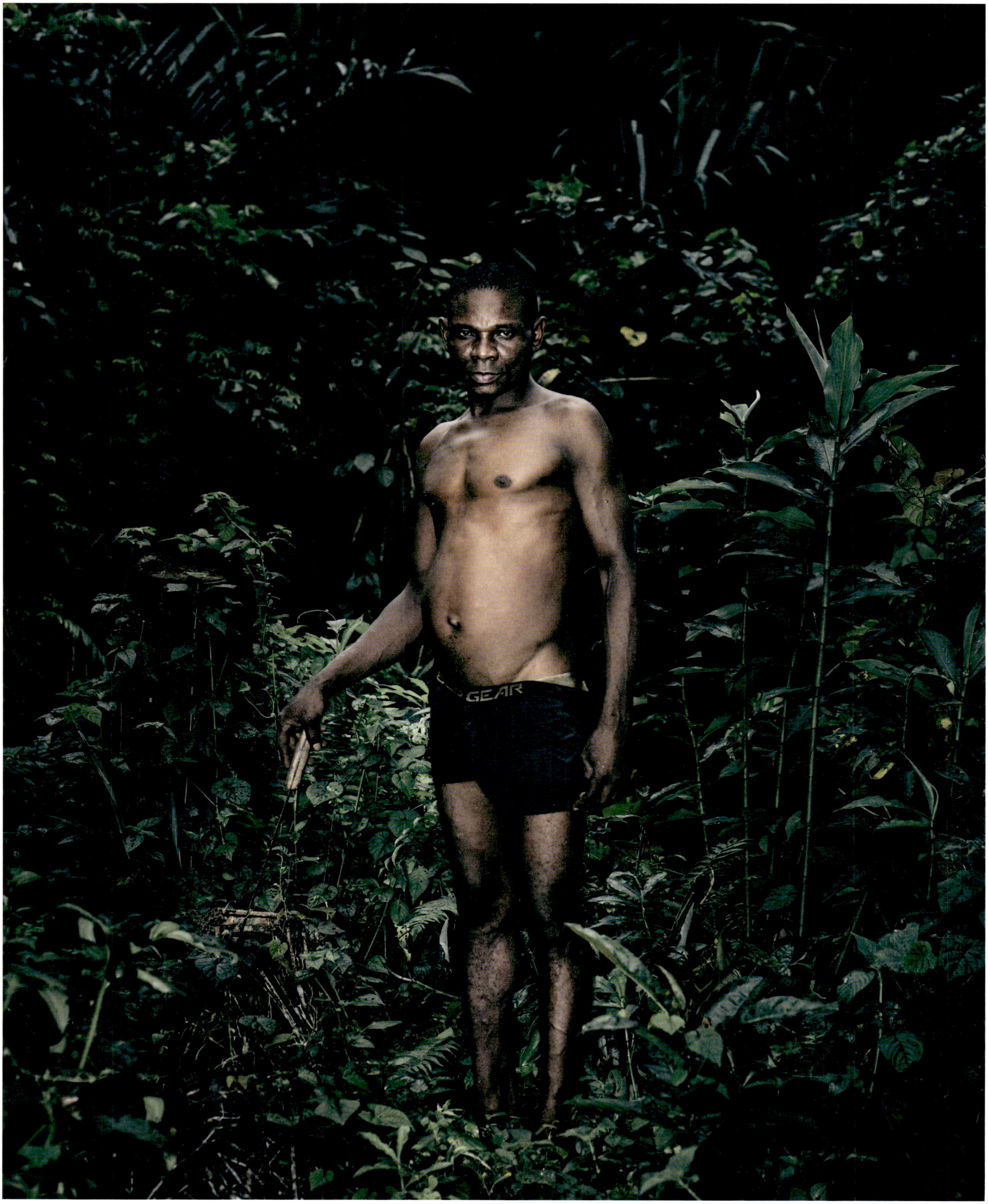
GEAR

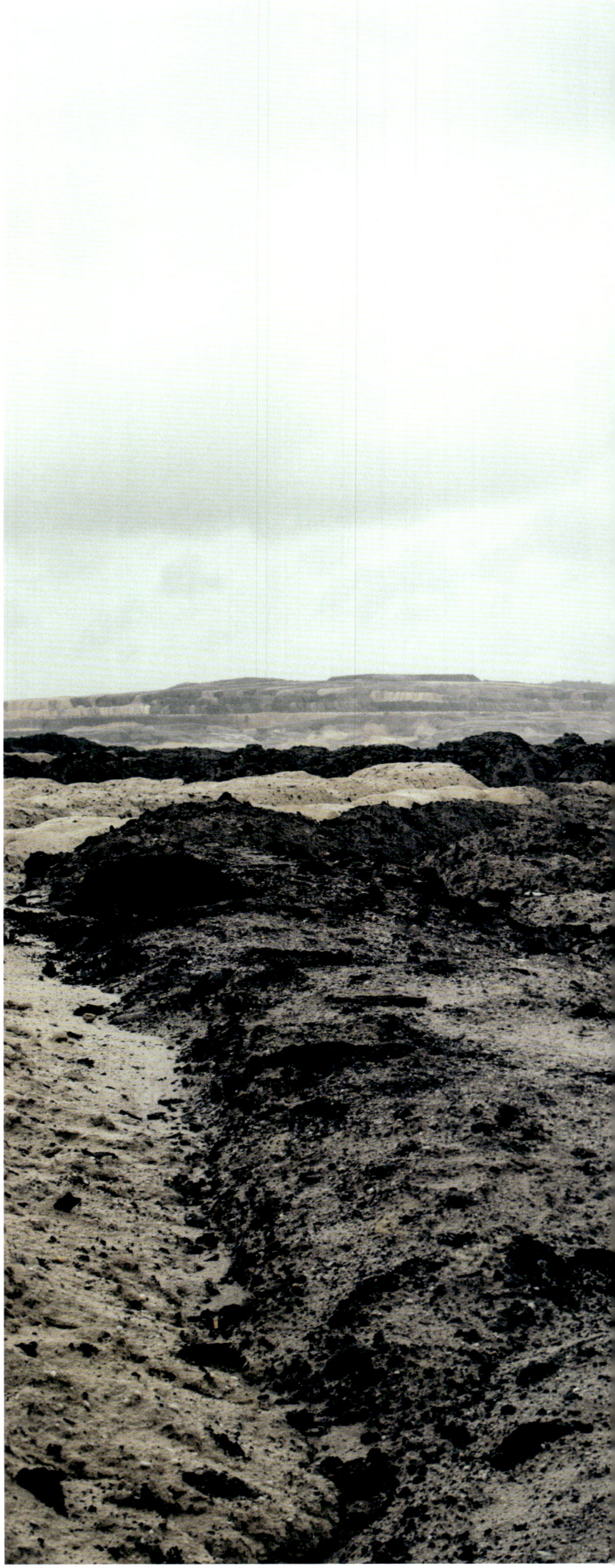

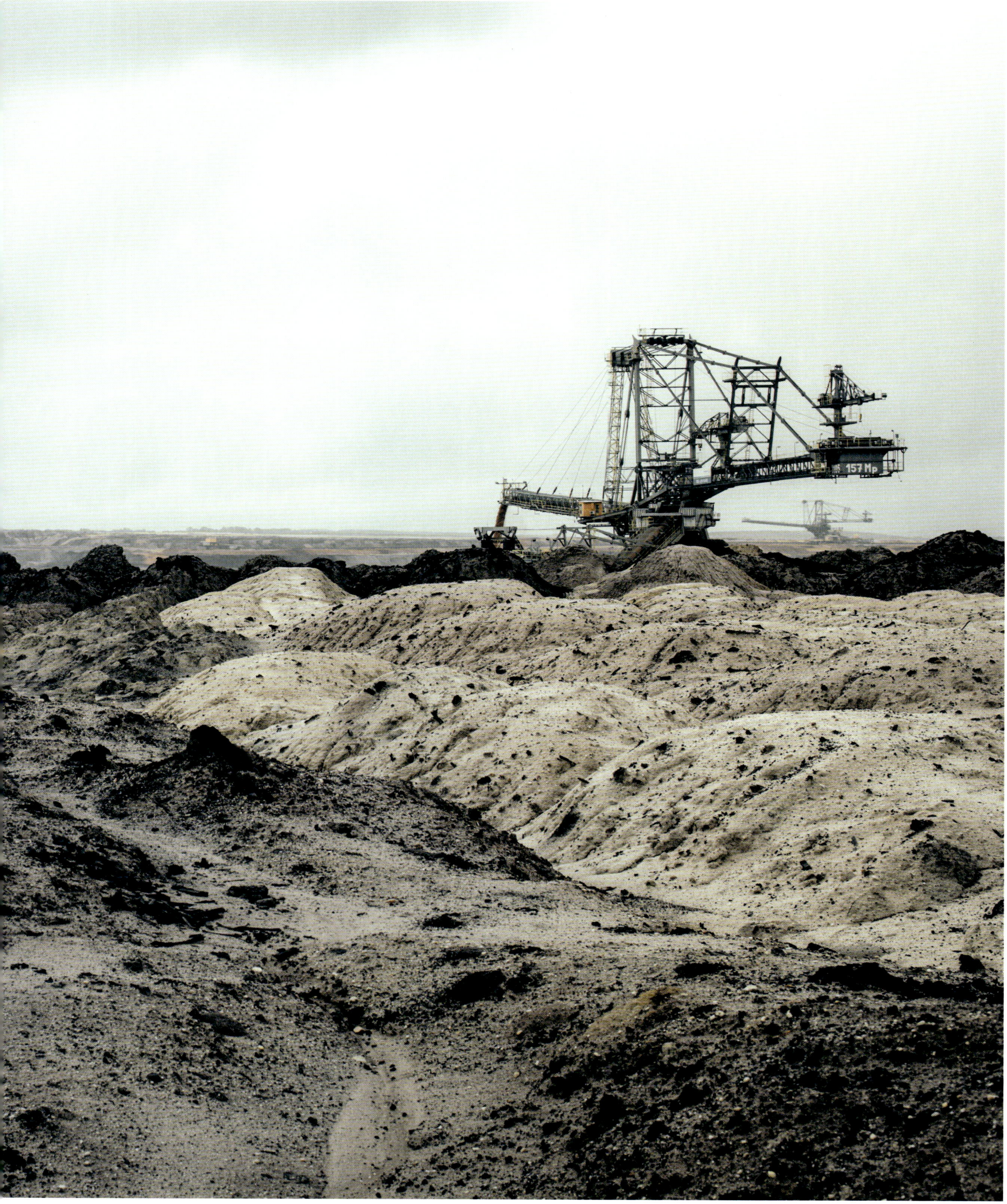
157 Mp

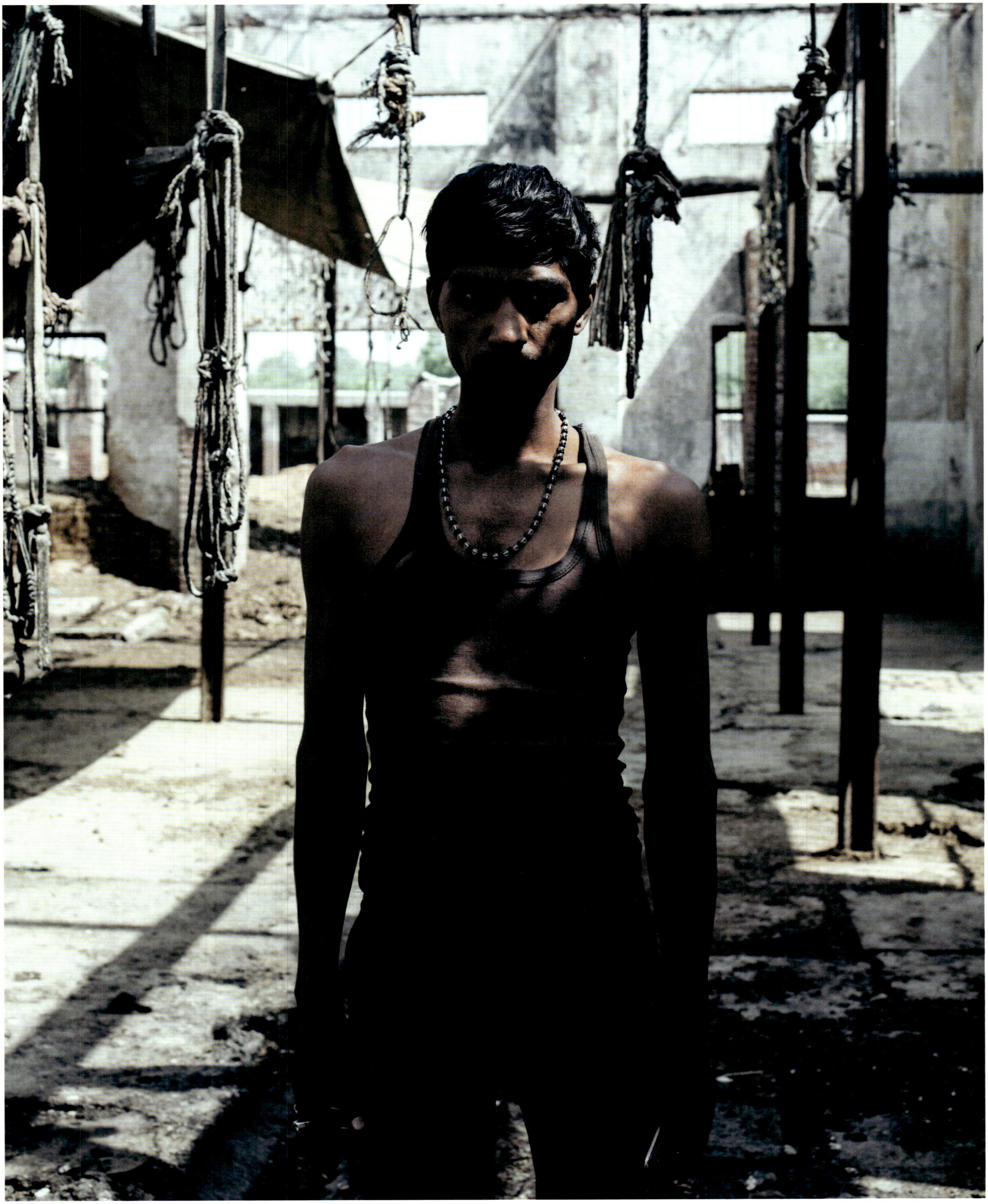

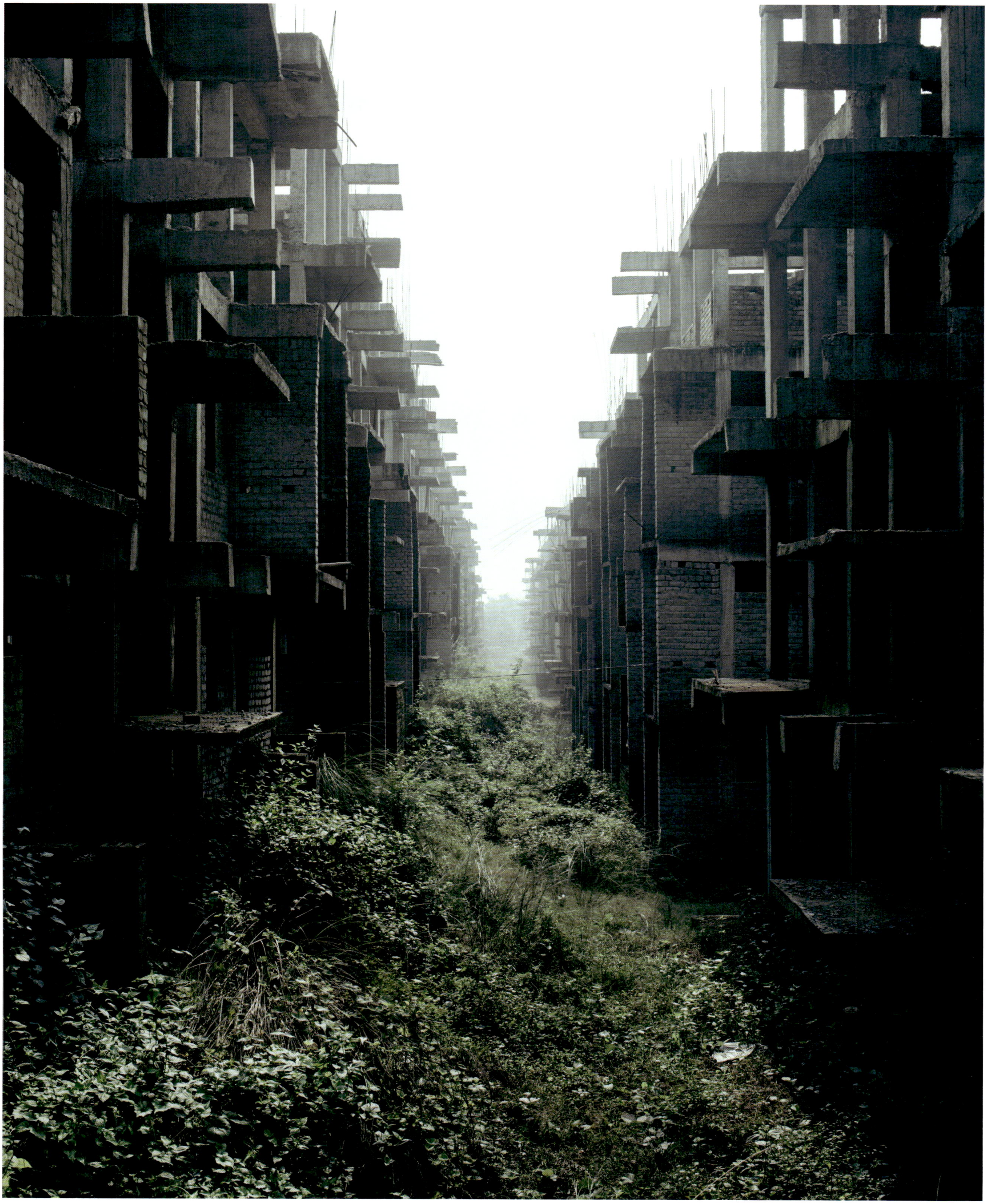

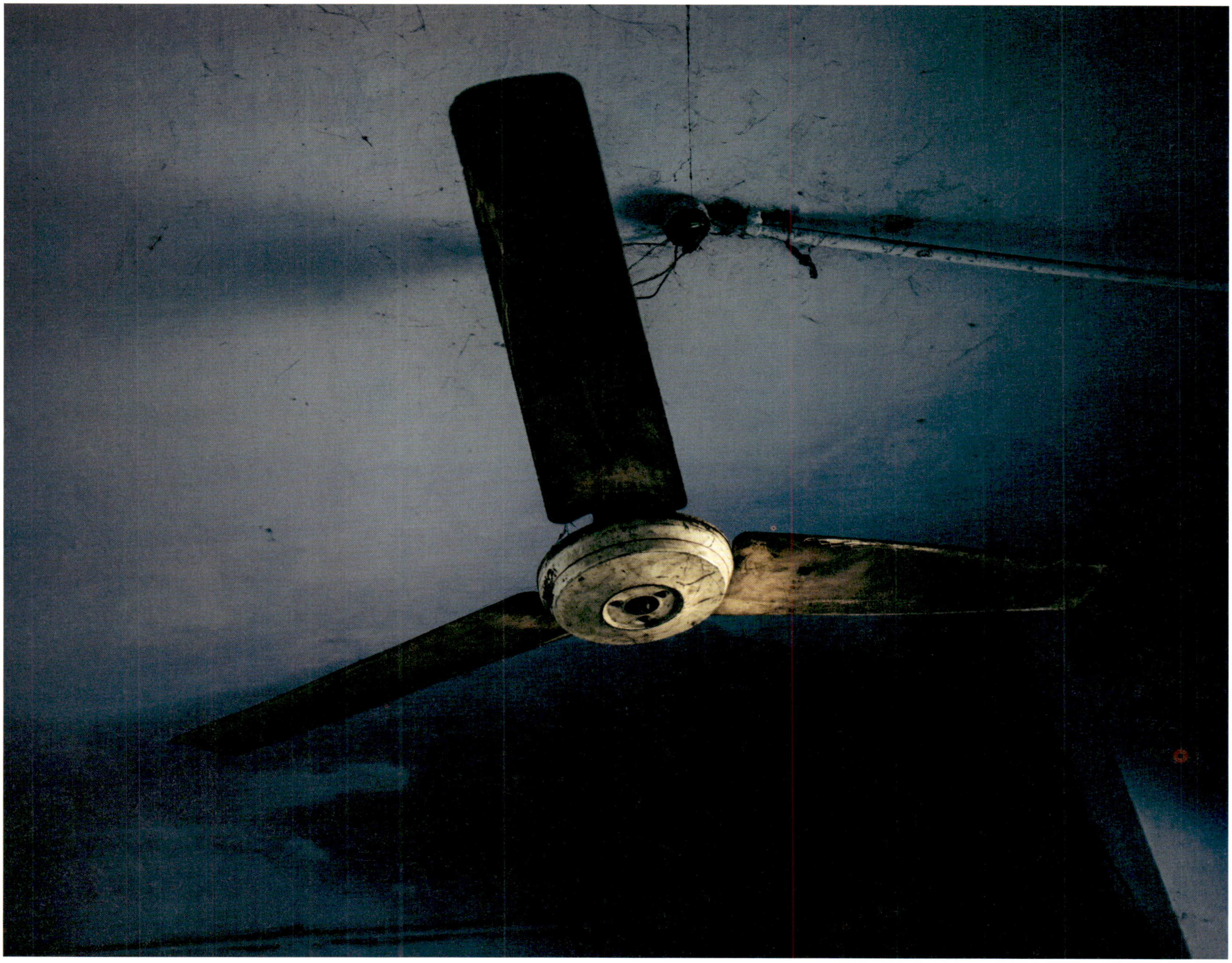

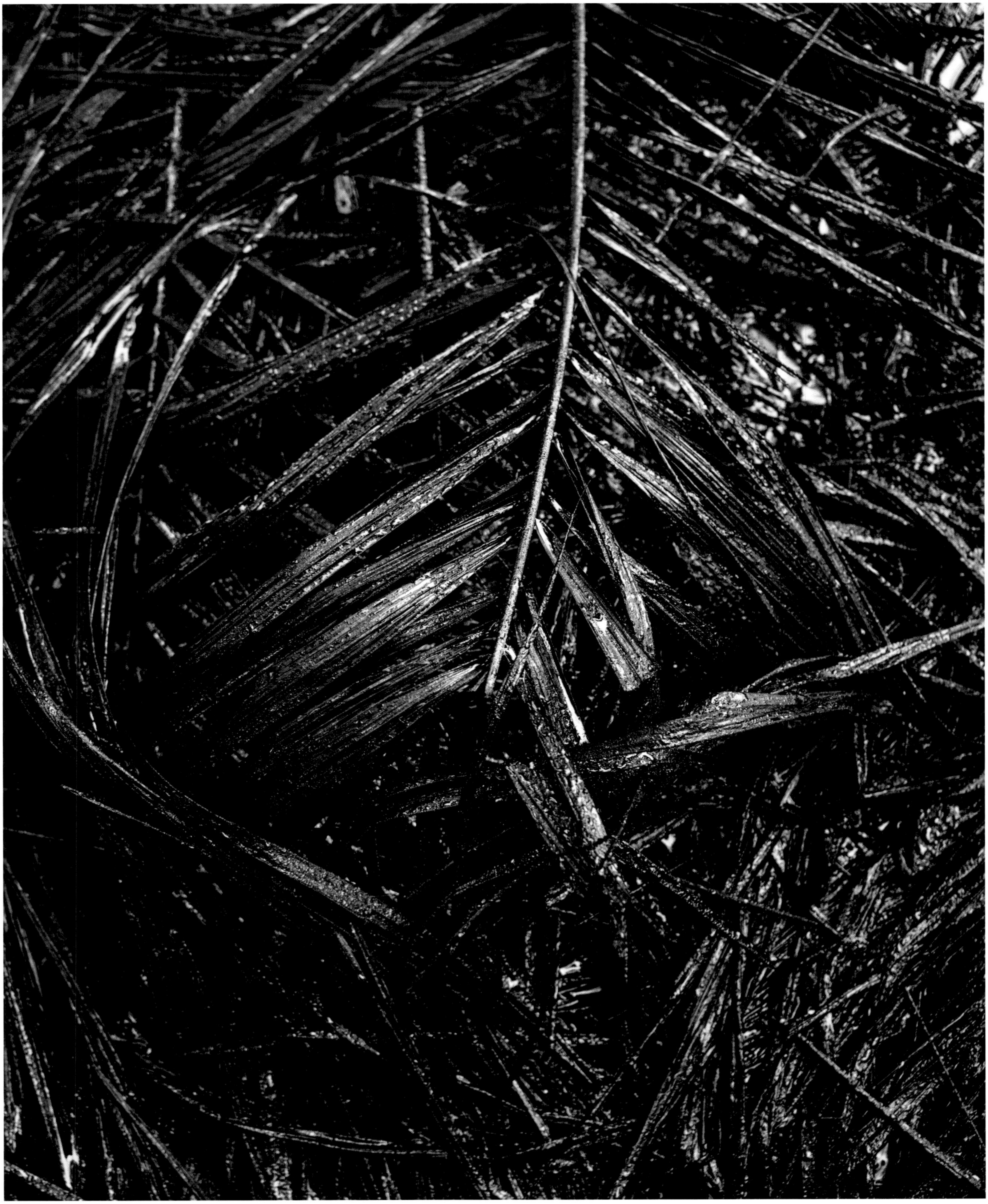

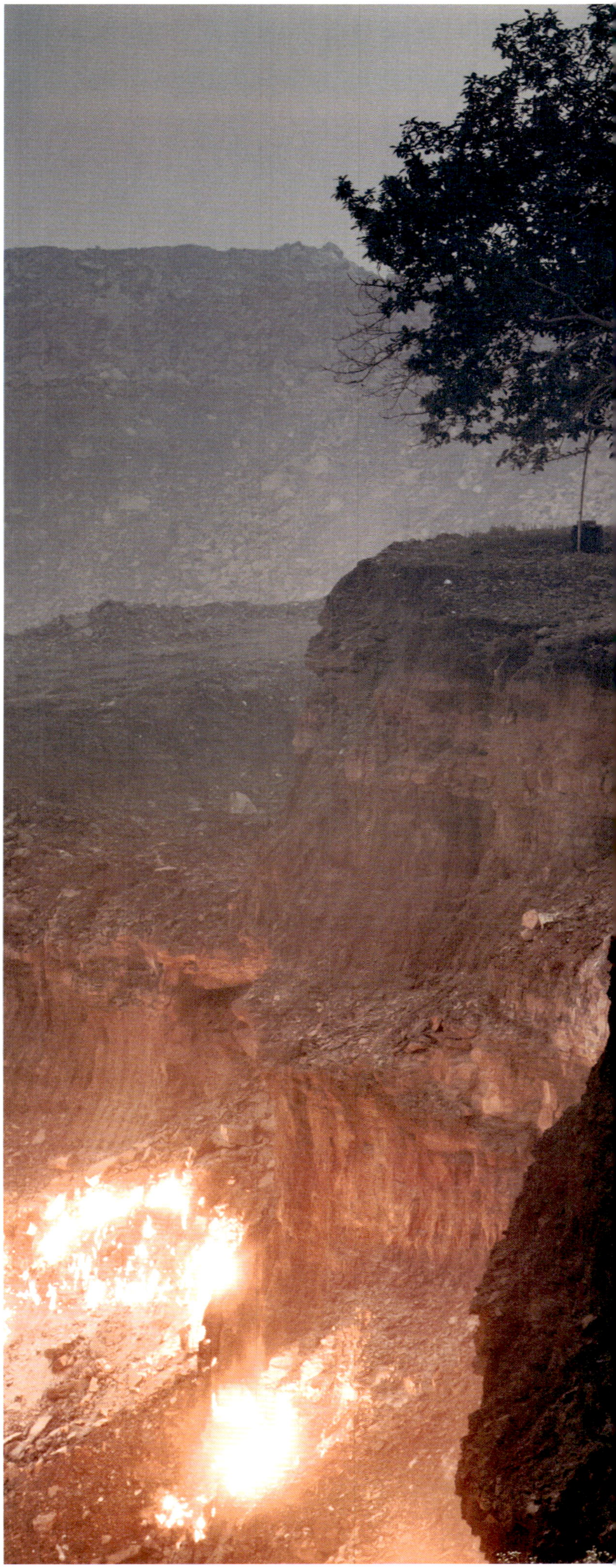

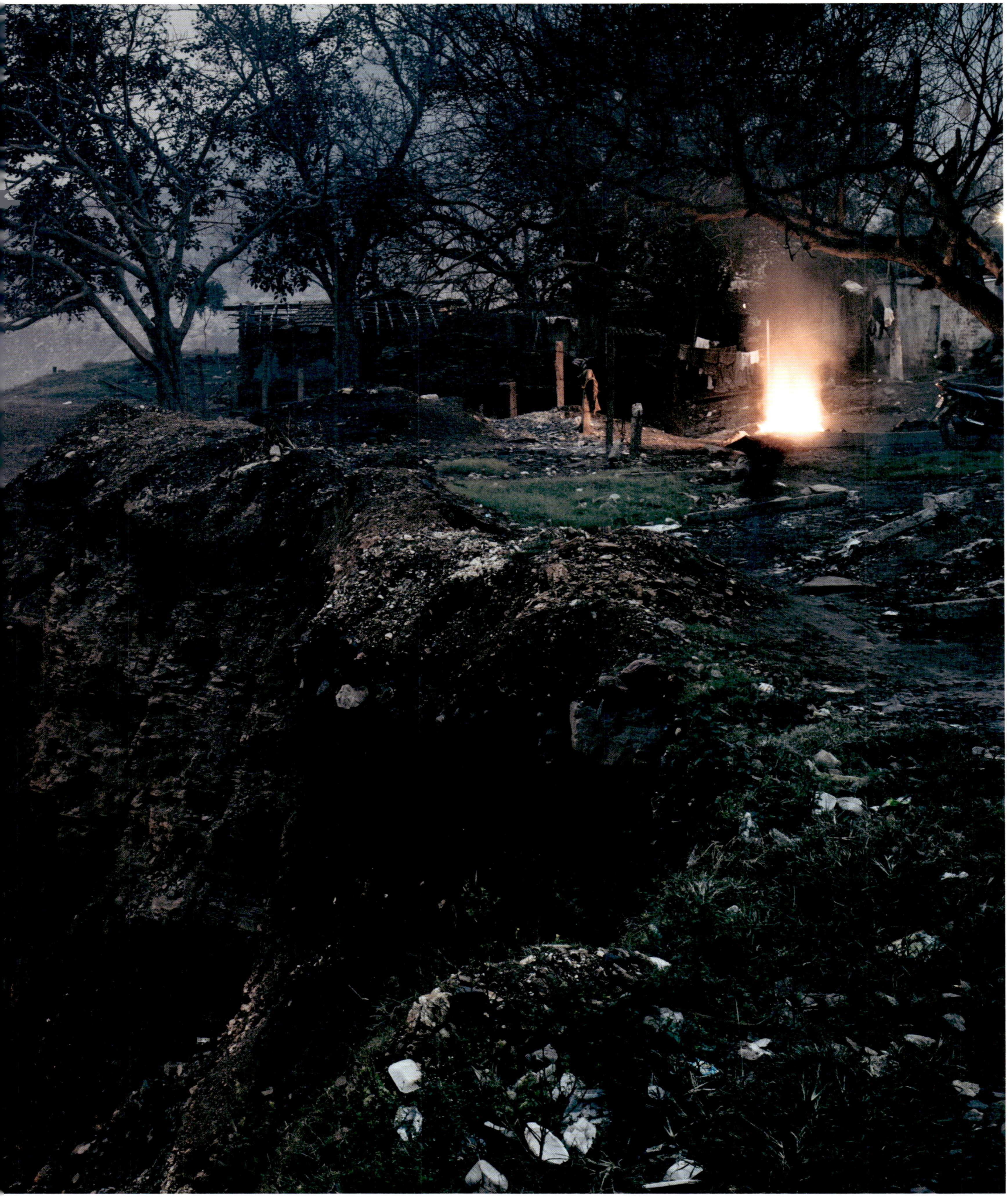

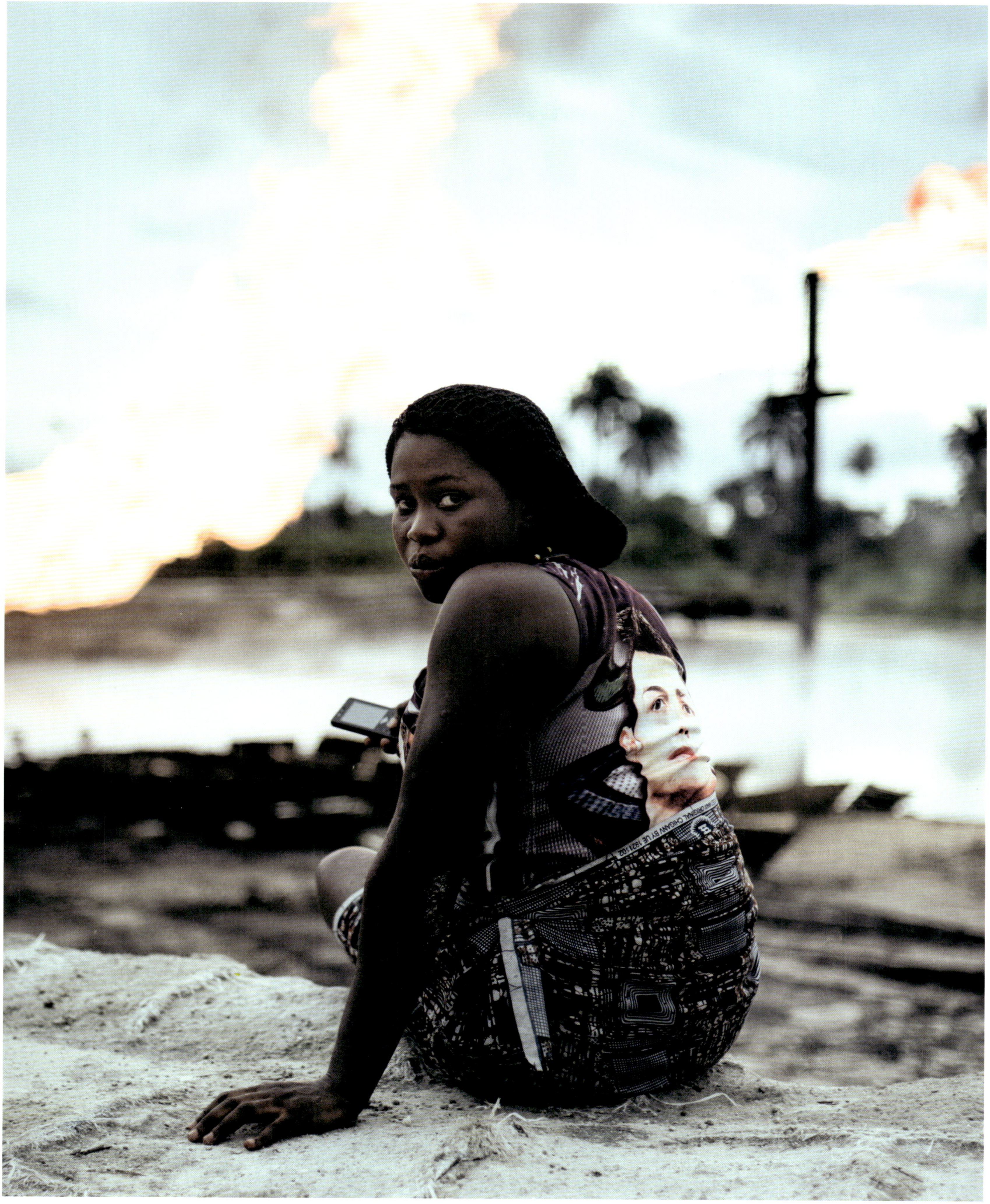

WAHALA. ON THE BRINK OF COLLAPSE.

Moritz Frischkorn

The apocalypse, popular imagination believes, will look like a kind of fire storm. Forests will burn, fertile land will be turned into desert, steam will rise from the earth. This well-known Hollywood iconography, circulating widely in film and mainstream media, creates feelings both of anxiety and excitement. It often comes with a special dramaturgy: at the very last moment, someone—mostly white, male, and muscular, with a college degree, or a bunch of consultants—arrives at the scene and performs some kind of heroic act. He turns the wheel around.

Catastrophe as catharsis, and a new morning rises. Who would not want to believe there was another day in paradise? But, already, the planet is on fire. Energy, stored for millennia within the earth's crust, is being burnt at a record speed. Fire is raging in different places all over the globe. As they say: the wrong Amazon is burning. Even in the Northern Hemisphere people are starting to acknowledge the climate crisis, as warmer summers, less rain and more arid afternoons are making themselves felt. Contrary to popular imagination, the apocalypse does not take the form of an event. It is an ongoing process, accelerating incrementally so that we all get used to it. But this is not entirely true: only if the fire does not burn your backyard can you afford to succumb to this process of numbing adaptation without thinking about where the fire actually comes from.

Maybe a veil needs to be taken off. While more and more people become aware that we are collectively putting at risk the future of our planet, fewer of us pay attention to the actual infrastructure that fossil fuel industries have built over the last 150 years and the way it impacts land and people. In the Nigerian Niger Delta, for example, leakages within the extensive networks of overland pipelines which connect the many small wellheads to the coastal ports have nearly completely destroyed the once fertile and rich ecosystem of mangrove forests. Ongoing poor maintenance coupled with repeated oil theft, for which pipelines are busted, have made life almost impossible. As a consequence, young men—jobless and without perspective—are forced to intensify their involvement in small-scale theft and production of illegally refined oil on small islands within the extensive side-arms of the delta.

Fossil fuel infrastructures are manifold and extend well into our immediate environment. From wellheads, oil pipelines, coal mines, tunnels and elevators, these channels of fire fork, branch out and merge back into large bunkering facilities, refineries, power plants, and filling stations. Finally, they reach the tanks of our cars, the smaller gas pipelines of our houses, the electricity with which we charge our phones. In fact, the massive activity of burning fossil fuels sticks, in one way or another, to anything we buy in the supermarket. Next to nothing would make it to the shelves without the fuel burnt in trucks, containerships and airplanes. Oil and coal are fueling a gigantic choreography of commodities and people, moving around the earth on an ever-greater scale and with ever more speed. Fossil fuels thus stick to our lives like a fine coating only visible in black light, a thin, invisible layer, viscous and almost impossible to wash off.

Architectural theorist Keller Easterling has shown that infrastructure space—the active form impacting both geography and behaviour—may well be the secret weapon of the powerful, the agent of profit and slow destruction.[1] And, really: Besides perhaps (tele)communication technologies, the information travelling in and out of our lives, nothing has altered our lives as thoroughly as fossil fuels. Its impact goes well beyond political ideologies or nation states. Many have noticed the finiteness of the modes of animation and the lifestyle that fossil fuel affords, yet collectively we seem to be neglecting the famous 'Limits of Growth.' It is, as if we believe there was, in fact, a Planet B. While we avert our eyes, land has and is already being remade at ever greater scales. If we took a closer look, we would see that the fire storm has ravaged many a land—houses are torn down once coal mines are abandoned in Eastern Germany, while new fires are lit at other sites, smoldering in Indian mountain ranges.

'What happens to the land, happens to the people,' theorist Linda Hogan reminds us.[2] While Western lifestyles have profited enormously from oil and coal being burnt endless people and beings continue to suffer from it. Today, the line between those forced to work within or next to the gigantic beast of the fossil fuel industry and those actually profiting from it without spending as much as a thought is manifold and porous. In China, the government has issued a new car model, which starts at $100,000 and is equipped with carbon filters and air cleaners. Owning this 'fabulous' vehicle means you can move from your house, which has filters, to your car, which has filters, to your work place, which has filters, and never get exposed to any environmental threat. That is, if you can pay for it.

While the destructive engine keeps on roaring, spilling flames into the sky, would we not do good to listen and learn from those that live on the other side of the car window, from those that dwell in the ruins of our Western lifestyle? Here or there, in that black space, submerged in a collective, you are never alone. In that underground, in the underbelly of consumerist over-mobility, in the undercommons, as Fred Moten and his collaborator Stefano Harney call it,[3] you may learn that it is not in your hands, in your pipelines, refineries, and combustion engines to ever hold the powers of the land. Property is replaced by an ethics of care, the individual intention by collective rehearsal. Where profit once reigned, powered by the normative position of the sovereign subject, there is chatter and sound. Where we once flew above the land, propelled by seemingly infinite energy, where we cut and opened it in endless fissures, wounding it until it bled, where we worked more than our fragile bodies would allow, driven by individual ambition, where we ate, consumed and incorporated more than we were able to digest, there now is a different energy, calm and sustained: a form of conviviality, of mutual aid and dependency, of care for one another and the many agents that make life possible.

In fact, in the undercommons, there is a very different kind of fire burning—it is the fire in the eyes of others, others that we love and care for. James Baldwin reminds us that this other fire—a social fire—puts us in relation with one another long before the current fantasies of total connectivity, accelerated mobility and hyper-extended supply chains.[4] Logistics, driven by fossil fuels, imagines itself as a choreographer, one that administers the most complex form of ballet 'played across oceans, borders and skies.'[5] But how could our conviviality take the form of a dance? To attain this 'standpoint of no standpoint,'[6] a possible first step would be to make an inventory of one's silent complicity in the ongoing neo-colonial exploitation of labour and land. A second step, maybe, would be a collective practice of mourning that very complicity, leaving behind with it the old sense of autonomous and forward-driven self. This form of emotional labour includes the realisation that warmth can not only be generated by burning fuel, but by mutual trust.

What form would photography then take? Maybe it would become more than mere representation of apocalypse, more of a call or invocation. At least, this is what I read in the eyes of Ese Awolowo. Her image is the last in the series of photographs by Robin Hinsch printed here. Ese Awolowo is sitting in front of a gas flaring site in Ughelli, Nigeria. She comes to the site twice a week to cook cassava chips. While her gaze is firm and almost accusatory, it also allows for another interpretation. It seems to me, as if Ese Awolowo offers us a last chance. How can we convince her not to turn her back on us? For on the back of the T-shirt she is wearing, there is the print of a white man: a mirror-image of those who profit from fossil fuel infrastructures while externalising its true costs. Does her gaze thus also ask us to reflect on our desire for the apocalypse quite differently? Why do we still revel at fire on the screen, why do we enjoy watching catastrophes from a safe distance, when we actually know that they are taking place at this moment, just around the corner? Those waiting for a Hollywood hero to save them, the picture tells us, will be left without company, all by themselves, with only their mirror image to contemplate.

1 Easterling, K. (2014). *Extrastatecraft: The Secret Power of Infrastructure Space*, London: Verso.
2 Cf. Ray, G. (2014). 'Writing the Ecocide-Genocide Knot Indigenous Knowledge and Critical Theory in the Endgame,' documenta14.de.
3 Harney, S. and Moten, F. (2014). *The Undercommons: Fugitive Planning &Black Study*, New York/Port Watson: Minor Compositions.
4 Baldwin, J. (2021). *Nothing Personal: An Essay*, Chicago: Beacon Press.
5 UPS (2012). *We Love Logistics*, TV commercial, cited after: Lecavalier, J. (2012). 'The restlessness of objects. Choreographing fulfillment,' in: *CABINET* 47, p. 90.
6 Harney, S. and Moten, F. (2014). *The Undercommons: Fugitive Planning &Black Study*, New York/Port Watson: Minor Compositions, p. 93.

IN ARCADIA

Sophie-Charlotte Opitz

And longer fall the shadows from the mountains high.
Virgil

When trying to define integrity, we usually think of our own all-encompassing ideals, which we are capable of implementing in harmony with the realities of life. The most important condition for this is the integrity of one's own body and mind. The individualism implicit in this basic humanistic idea is hardly surprising, since we form our thoughts about the world in our head. It is from there that we perceive, focus on events, analyse circumstances, weigh different options, and arrive at judgments. But as the philosopher Judith Butler already noted, the precariousness of our integrity should be recognised as 'a shared condition of human life'[1] and not only be understood as an individual problem. In the course of asking well-warranted questions about who develops a sense of duty when faced with this generalised vulnerability of existence and how, Butler pleads for a new understanding of responsibility, one that is globally conceived and resists practices of imperialist appropriation. The violated individual is thus a violated part of the world. Conversely, this also means that we must protect others in order to preserve our own integrity.

These thoughts are already addressed by the title of Robin Hinsch's project *Wahala*. The Yoruba word means 'problem' or 'stress,' and in Nigeria it is used as a pidgin term commonly understood by different ethnic groups. It rarely stands alone, but when it does, it means there is a problem that leaves one shaken and speechless. In Hinsch's project, speechlessness arises in the face of the subject's complexity, which points to the global extent of 'affectedness' in order to show that 'their' problem is our problem.

Taking a transnational perspective, *Wahala* addresses the production conditions of fossil fuel extraction and the related cultural history of Western appropriation. In the process, it visualises the resulting destructive mechanisms connected to the exploitation of the global South. The scope of devastation revealed in the project illustrates that environmental violation not only ends up wrecking the habitats of humans and animals, but also the integrity of cultural practice.

Hinsch photographs landscapes and people in India, Nigeria, Poland, and Germany. His images are atmospheric, simultaneously familiar and foreign, intimate and unfamiliar. He shifts back and forth between details and overviews: wide landscape scenes of deep gorges and dark abysses meet close-ups of coal lumps and burnt flora; ephemeral clouds of smoke and glistening fires meet dilapidated industrial facilities and fields covered with pools of oil shimmering blue. This fragmentary gaze does not distinguish between 'here' and 'there' or 'us' and 'them.' And thus the viewers can't quite be sure of where exactly they are looking.

Hinsch deliberately works with the instability of the visible. Here, he forms a dialectic in space in the sense elaborated by sociologist Henri Lefebvre—one that concretises social dichotomies of exchange and use between dynamic global networks and static sites of production and consumption.[2] Space is simultaneously concrete and abstract: concrete, in that the places included within it can still be localised; abstract, in that their economic contexts persist, regardless of local changes. Hinsch's use of photography—a medium that is per se incomplete—materialises this dialectic and points out that even though fragments and overviews can never do justice to each other, complex global issues can still be negotiated within the image. The inherent gaps of photography with all its visual uncertainties are no longer defined as the medium's drawback, but offer an opportunity for activating one's own thoughts and subsequent actions.

Contrary to the idea that landscapes are merely the backdrops for human action, the stage of our sheer existence, *Wahala* presents landscapes as an inherent part of cultural practice. W.J.T. Mitchell also argues that 'landscape' should be understood less as a noun and more as a verb.[3] We do not simply act in the landscape; the landscape also interacts with us.

In the project, this becomes clear, among other things, in the close-up of a rusty storage tank in the Niger Delta. Three holes roughly hammered into the metal gape like the fangs of a shark, splitting the surface and giving a glimpse into the supposed interior—a black void. Like many other storage tanks, the local crude oil from Bodo was stored in it, and from there the oil was sent abroad for further processing.

These processes damage the biotope of the Niger Delta in a variety of ways: the appropriation of resources and their export economically weakens the country on a massive scale. The expansion of oil exploration is destroying the terrain as it occupies the geographical space. Furthermore, wear-related leaks and fires contaminate the soil and water resources in the Niger region. In addition, flaring of the gas released by oil extraction damages the flora and fauna by emitting toxic substances, such as sulfur dioxide and methane, and releasing carcinogenic particles. Agriculture, fishing, and livestock farming are now only possible under massive restrictions.

What we see in the photograph of the three holes in the storage tank is thus an attempt to make a living in a place that is unlivable. In the process, the lack of opportunities for securing a sustainable livelihood often leads the inhabitants to crime, like the illegal oil extraction documented here. At these ramshackle storage sites, which cut through the landscape, wreck habitats, and undermine a sustainable local economy, a product suitable for the (black) market can be extracted, which makes certain parts of the population able to temporarily maintain their income, and thus their lives.

These mechanisms create a vicious cycle, since the local people who suffer from poor living conditions as a result of fossil fuel extraction further contribute to the intensification of natural disaster with these actions born of necessity. Among other things, the storage tanks torn open in this makeshift way release hundreds of liters of crude oil, which further pollute the environment. The inhabitants themselves become perpetrators, further damaging the landscape that defines their homeland.

This mutual appropriation of the mechanisms of exploitation can be seen continuously throughout *Wahala*. Here, the dialogue between the photographs creates a space which interweaves the many narratives of the people and the landscape, of the exploited and the exploiters, of progress and stasis.

Tragedy becomes evident in the power structures that create this dualism in the realities of life, which the images reveal. We behold deserted spoil tips and coal seams, signs of capitalist prosperity, progress, and growth. At the same time, the large corporations' hegemonic claim on visibility is continuously disrupted by references to the inhabitants' actions: small stalls offering self-refined diesel and heating oil for sale in a mishmash of plastic bottles; young women smuggling lumps of coal away from the mining areas; fireplaces where makeshift coke refining is carried out. These people occupy the occupied; they form a parallel society that takes advantage of exploration due to a lack of prospects, yet they also find themselves dependent on those mechanisms in the process.

A photograph shows the last ruins of an abandoned village in Dhanbad, India, which has almost completely fallen into the edge of a spoil tip. Much like the case of oil extraction in the Niger Delta, the civilian population, which is offered little to no compensation for sacrificing their homes to coal mining, is dependent on the resource. Here too, people reproduce the mechanism of exploitation through illegal private coal mining. And for this reason, they have to stay close to the coal mine and create short-term habitats—short-term because the mining area continues eating through the landscape, also consigning future homes to the abyss of the dumps one day.

The photograph from Dhanbad, like many other photographs in the project, resonates with the art historical discourse of Romantic and Baroque ruin paintings. Much like the images of Claude Lorrain, Nicolas Poussin, and William Turner, the ruins in *Wahala* symbolise transience. At the same time, they formulate a critique of imperialist systems of domination: as image and inversion of the neoliberal ideal—the freedom of boundless economic growth—these tokens of finitude manifest the decay of human civilization. These ruins, wastelands, and deserts herald the decline of a supposedly advanced civilization, in which a system of energy extraction wrecks every living space and ultimately destroys itself in the long run. Similar to Arcadia, the symbol of the Golden Age, happiness and death form a union, in which the landscapes photographed serve as the starting and end point of all existence.

In addition to spaces, *Wahala* also merges different times. Beginning and end can no longer be separated. This is impressively visualised in the images of fire that one encounters throughout the project. In India, the coal industry is a testimony to British imperialism. Mining also began in Jharia in 1894. Today, the region is one of India's largest and most important suppliers of coal. The first documented fire broke out there in 1916—and is still burning today. A photograph shows the gorges of Jharia dominated by blazing flames. The inhabitants' temporary huts stand at the edges. What looks like a campfire in the middle of the huts turns out to be the same fire as the one in the gorge. It eats through the layers of sediment, making no distinction between here and there or then and now. The singular event of the 1916 fire has now transformed into an everlasting, ubiquitous state. This is the feature that makes this project unique: by making the passive 'condition' visible, *Wahala* transforms it back into an active 'event,'an occurrence seen and perceived throughout many photographs. Detached from temporal or local limitations, it is thus reframed as an experience in the original sense of the German *Ereignis*: an observed event that is by definition characterised by change.

Fog, smoke, and fire recur everywhere in *Wahala*. They cover the ground, billow through the fields, and veil the landscapes they occupy. In the Niger Delta, it comes through the flaring of the natural gas associated with oil extraction, which yields toxic fumes. This simultaneously creates non-places[4]—places that have been stripped of their cultural significance—and un-places—places where cultural life is no longer possible. As described earlier on, the integrity of cultural practice is violated as a result. In several of the images, large slabs of cassava are laid out around the gas fires. Traders put them there to increase their production capacity, as the rapid drying lets them to get their goods to market faster. But even though the process is more efficient, toxic fumes permeate the food in the process, and the cassava is contaminated before it is consumed. Destruction thus takes place from without and within. The former symbiosis between nature and culture disintegrates: the cultural practice of humans harms nature, and nature poisons humans in turn.

Wahala translates the violence of these global mechanisms of fossil fuel extraction into visibilities that help us grasp their complexity. The project resists temporal linearity and understands bodies in the sense articulated by Gilles Deleuze, that is not as organically human, but as abstract and ubiquitous.[5] Now we can understand: with the exploitation of the planet, we destroy ourselves.

At the end, the cassava trader Ese Awolowo looks us straight in the eye. In the moment of looking at the photograph, Ese's gaze connects with ours; beginning and end, cause and effect, past and future collapse into each other. What remains is a fragile present whose vulnerability must serve as the compass of our actions.

1 Butler, J. (2009). *Frames of War*. London: Verso, p. 13.
2 Lefebvre, H. (1991). *The Production of Space*. Oxford: Blackwell, pp. 341-342.
3 Mitchell, W. J. T. (2002). *Landscape and Power*. Chicago: The University of Chicago Press, p. 1.
4 Augé, M. (1995). *Non-places: Introduction to an Anthropology of Supermodernity*. London: Verso.
5 Deleuze, G. (2004). *A Thousand Plateaus: Capitalism and Schizophrenia*. London, New York: Continuum, p. 34.

01 Unicorn, Tarkwa Bay, Lagos, Nigeria, 2019
03 Unknown Worker I, Makoko, Lagos, Nigeria, 2019
05 Sabitri Kumani, Jharia, Dhanbad, Jharkhand, India, 2019
06 Roman Janiszek, Wałbrzych, Lower Silesia, Poland, 2020
10 Gas Flaring Site, Ughelli, Niger Delta, Nigeria, 2019
13 Suhani Kumari, Jharia, Dhanbad, Jharkhand, India, 2019
14 Coal Field Fire I, Jharia, Dhanbad, Jharkhand, India, 2019
17 Compressor Station, Mallnow, Brandenburg, Germany, 2022
18 Reuben Ayuba and Friend, Luekue, Niger Delta, Nigeria, 2019
21 Temple Bell, Jharia, Dhanbad, Jharkhand, India, 2019
23 Protestor's Treehouses, Hambach Forest, North Rhine-Westphalia, Germany, 2020
25 Polluted Area in B-Dere, Niger Delta, Nigeria, 2019
27 Auf dem Goldacker, Abandoned House, Morschenich, North Rhine-Westphalia, Germany, 2020
29 Holy Cow, Dhanbad, Jharkhand, India, 2019
30 Coking Area I, Jharia, Dhanbad, Jharkhand, India, 2019
31 Coking Area II, Jharia, Dhanbad, Jharkhand, India, 2019
32 Charles Olufemi, Fire Junction, Ijegun, Lagos State, Nigeria, 2019
35 Schwarze Pumpe, Brandenburg, Spremberg, Germany, 2016
37 Joy, Bariga, Lagos, Nigeria, 2019
39 Sleeping Dog, Jharia, Dhanbad, Jharkhand, India, 2019
40 Open Cast Mine Inden, Krauthausen, North Rhine-Westphalia, Germany, 2020
43 Unknown Man I, B-Dere, Niger Delta, Nigeria, 2019
45 Damaged Oil Tank, Bodo, Niger Delta, Nigeria, 2019
46 Abdulmumin Ibrahim and Rafiu Bankole, Lagos, Nigeria, 2019
49 Abandoned Ship, Bodo, Niger Delta, Nigeria, 2019
51 Gaushala, Haryana, India, 2017
53 Coking Area III, Jharia, Dhanbad, Jharkhand, India, 2019
55 Roman Janiszek's Pickaxe, Wałbrzych, Lower Silesia, Poland, 2020
57 Abandoned St. Albanus and Leonhardus, Manheim, North Rhine-Westphalia, Germany, 2020
59 Unknown Worker II, Makoko, Lagos, Nigeria, 2019
60 Chief Damian Vidag-Kobani, Goi Community, Niger Delta, Nigeria, 2019.
63 Merchant, Makoko, Lagos, Nigeria, 2019
65 Piece of Coal, Jharia, Dhanbad, Jharkhand, India, 2019
66 Opencast Mine Reichwalde, Lausitz, Saxonia, Germany, 2020
68 Unknown Man II, Jharia, Dhanbad, Jharkhand, India, 2019
71 Polluted Area in B-Dere II, Niger Delta, Nigeria, 2019
73 Destroyed House, Jharia, Dhanbad, Jharkhand, India, 2019
75 Distillery, Luekue Bangha, River State, Niger Delta, Nigeria, 2019
77 Friday Nwiee, Luekue Bangha, River State, Niger Delta, Nigeria, 2019
79 Masked Girl I, Jharia, Dhanbad, Jharkhand, India, 2019
80 Coal Smoke, Jharia, Dhanbad, Jharkhand, India, 2019
83 Burnt Oil Tanker, Fire Junction, Ijegun, Lagos State, Nigeria, 2019
85 Hindu Temple, Jharia, Dhanbad, Jharkhand, India, 2019
87 Steelmerchant, Scrap Market, Owode Onirin Market, Lagos State, Nigeria, 2019.
88 Abandoned Autobahn, Manheim, North Rhine-Westphalia, Germany, 2020
91 Demolished House, Manheim, North Rhine-Westphalia, Germany, 2020
93 Opencast Mine, Jharia, Dhanbad, Jharkhand, India, 2019
95 Abayomi Akintayo, Bariga, Lagos, Nigeria, 2019
97 Gas Flaring Site II, Ughelli, Niger Delta, Nigeria, 2019
99 Late Chief John Baribor Dooh, Goi, Niger Delta, Nigeria, 2019
100 Plastic Collector, Port Harcourt, Niger Delta, Nigeria, 2019
102 Neha Kumari, Jharia, Dhanbad, Jharkhand, India, 2019
103 Unfinished House, Belgaria, Dhanbad, Jharkhand, India, 2019
105 Burnt Cars, Fire Junction, Ijegun, Lagos State, Nigeria, 2019
106 Unknown Worker III, Autoparts Market, Owode Onirin Market, Lagos State, Nigeria, 2019.
107 Informal Petrol Station, Port Harcourt, River State, Nigeria, 2019
109 Leyira Nwako, Luekue Bangha, River State, Niger Delta, Nigeria, 2019
110 Opencast Mine, Jänschwalde, Lausitz, Brandenburg, Germany, 2016
112 Unknown Worker V, Haryana, India, 2019
113 Unfinished Settlement, Belgaria, Dhanbad, Jharkhand, India, 2019
115 Mine Office, Jharia, Dhanbad, Jharkhand, India, 2019
116 Polluted Soil, Bodo, Niger Delta, Nigeria, 2019
118 Coal Field Fire II, Jharia, Dhanbad, Jharkhand, India, 2019
121 Ese Awolowo, Ughelli, Niger Delta, Nigeria, 2019

Local Producers in India and Nigeria

Pinaki Roy is a teacher and social activist working at the Jharia coalfield in India. He is the intiator of Coalfields Children Classes, a special educational project for the children of coal scavengers' families. His goal is, with the help of his twenty-five years of experience as a teacher, to enable children to discover a perspective beyond coal-related professions for themselves. Since 1999, Pinaki Roy has conducted a variety of creative and social projects under the umbrella of the Institution for National Amity.

Fyneface Dumnamene Fyneface is an environmental justice activist, human rights defender and the executive director of Youths and Environmental Advocacy Centre (YEAC), a non-governmental and non-profit organisation based in the Niger Delta region of Nigeria, West Africa. In his activism and social campaigns, he focuses and campaigns on environment, livelihoods and indigenous rights; climate action and forest conservation; human rights and peace-building; education and empowerment; gender, maternal health and sanitation; youths and non-violent advocacy as well as anti-corruption and good governance. Fyneface uses the Do No Harm, gender and human rights-based approaches and research data-driven advocacy in his social campaigns with regular weekly live appearances on radio to reach millions of people in the Niger Delta.

Nnenna Obibuaku is a freelance journalist and multimedia professional with over sixteen years of experience. Currently, she works as a producer throughout the African continent with a particular focus on Nigeria. Prior to this role, she was a producer and manager of the British Broadcasting Corporation in Lagos, Nigeria.

Authors

Moritz Frischkorn is an artist and researcher based in Berlin. His practice unfolds non-human choreographies and their socio-political effects in different societal fields such as public space, social protest, and logistics. He produces research-based live performances, writes, curates, and teaches. His PhD thesis entitled 'More-Than-Human Choreography' will be published with [transcript] in 2023.

Dr. Sophie Charlotte Opitz holds a doctorate in art and media studies. As a curator and collection manager at various international institutions, she has realised a large number of exhibitions to date and regularly publishes articles in specialist and photography books and catalogues. She has been awarded the Thomas Mann Fellowship for 2023. Her research interests include global image hegemonies and visual cultures of memory.

Wahala was initiated as part of the artistic-research project entitled *The Great Report* by Moritz Frischkorn. Based on the observation that logistics companies sometimes call themselves 'choreographers,' the project unfolds how global supply chains create links between distant publics while reproducing neocolonial inequalities. The project, co-produced by Kampnagel, Hamburg premiered on 16 January 2020. An ongoing online-archive exists at www.greatreport.net.

My sincere thanks to Liberty Adrian, Christoph Albrecht, Abdulmumin Ibrahim, Rafiu Bankole Jona Caspar Bähr, Janusz Beck, Michael Biedowicz, Melike Bilir, Frederik Busch, Julia Dautel, Boris Füting, Gerlind Ehlert, Julia Maiquez Esterlich, Bettina Freimann, Moritz Frischkorn, Fyneface Dumname Fyneface, Charlotte Gosch, Fritz Habekuss, Lorenz Hartwig, Helge Hasselberg, Hella Hinsch, Hans Hinsch, Hermes Iyele, Annalena Kirchler, Carol Körting, Ulrike Kremeier, Tobias Laukemper, Prof. Vincent Kohlbecher, Matthias Fritz Königschulte, Igor Carlavitch Guedes Kramer, Marcin Krasnowolski, Florentine Muhry, Jan-Philipp Neumann, Nnenna Obibuaku, Busayo Olowu, Tife Owolabi, Pinaki Roy, Heidi Schnee, Prof. Almut Schneider, Prof. Linn Schröder, Julie-Ann Shiraishi, Trine Skraastad, Fynn Steiner, Sadhana Stülpnagel, Dr. Sophie-Charlotte Opitz, Nina Venus and everybody who was involved in this project. Initial dummy designed by Studio Otherypes.

Wahala was gratefully supported by the following institutions:
Behörde für Kultur und Medien Hamburg
Elbkulturfonds
Ifa—Institut für Auslandaustausch
Hamburgische Kulturstiftung

Hamburg | Ministry of Culture and Media
Elbkulturfonds

ifa Institut für Auslandsbeziehungen

hamburgische kulturstiftung

Wahala
First published in 2022 by
GOST Books, London

info@gostbooks.com
gostbooks.com

Edited and designed by GOST:
Rossella Castello, Katie Clifford, Gemma Gerhard, Justine Hucker, Allon Kaye, Eleanor Macnair, Claudia Paladini, Ana Rocha

Image reproduction by Shifting Pixels:
Caroline Cortizo, Samantha Humble-Smith

Translations by Good and Cheap Art Translators:
Stanton Taylor

Printed in Italy by EBS

British Library cataloguing-in-publication data.
A catalogue record of this book is available from the British Library.

ISBN 978-1-910401-70-5